Cambridge Elements ≡

Elements in Publishing and Book Culture
edited by
Samantha Rayner
University College London
Leah Tether
University of Bristol

NEW ADULT FICTION

Jodi McAlister

Deakin University

CAMBRIDGE
UNIVERSITY PRESS

CAMBRIDGE
UNIVERSITY PRESS

University Printing House, Cambridge CB2 8BS, United Kingdom

One Liberty Plaza, 20th Floor, New York, NY 10006, USA

477 Williamstown Road, Port Melbourne, VIC 3207, Australia

314–321, 3rd Floor, Plot 3, Splendor Forum, Jasola District Centre,
New Delhi – 110025, India

103 Penang Road, #05–06/07, Visioncrest Commercial, Singapore 238467

Cambridge University Press is part of the University of Cambridge.

It furthers the University's mission by disseminating knowledge in the pursuit of
education, learning, and research at the highest international levels of excellence.

www.cambridge.org
Information on this title: www.cambridge.org/9781108827881
DOI: 10.1017/9781108900737

First published 2021

A catalogue record for this publication is available from the British Library.

ISBN 978-1-108-82788-1 Paperback
ISSN 2514-8524 (online)
ISSN 2514-8516 (print)

New Adult Fiction

Elements in Publishing and Book Culture

DOI: 10.1017/9781108900737

First published online: October 2021

Jodi McAlister

Deakin University

Author for correspondence: Jodi McAlister, jodi.mcalister@deakin.edu.au

ABSTRACT: The term 'new adult' was coined in 2009 by St Martin's Press, when it sought submissions for a contest for 'fiction similar to YA that can be published and marketed as adult – a sort of "older YA" or "new adult"'. However, the literary category that later emerged bore less resemblance to young adult fiction and instead became a subgenre of another major popular genre: romance. This Element uses new adult fiction as a case study to explore how genres develop in the twenty-first-century literary marketplace. It traces new adult's evolution through three key stages to demonstrate the fluidity that characterises contemporary genres. It argues for greater consideration of paratextual factors in studies of genre. Using a genre worlds approach, it contends that to productively examine genre, we must consider industrial and social factors as well as texts.

KEYWORDS: genre, literary classification, new adult, popular fiction, twenty-first-century publishing

ISBNs: 9781108827881 (PB), 9781108900737 (OC)
ISSNs: 2514-8524 (online), 2514-8516 (print)

Contents

Introduction

One of the first things I, like most other scholars, usually do when approaching a subject is to define specifically what I am writing about. After all, it is difficult to make any kind of substantive claims about something when what that thing is has not been clearly set out.

However, when I embarked on this project about new adult fiction, it quickly became clear that I would have to take a different approach. Since the term 'new adult' was coined by St Martin's Press in 2009, its meaning has changed so swiftly and so dramatically that to begin with a definition of the term would be to misrepresent it and to limit the usefulness of any kind of study of it.

It would also undersell what is arguably new adult's most interesting feature: its evolution as a genre. As I will go on to show in the following sections, what new adult means has shifted dramatically over the decade or so that it has existed. The term clearly has staying power, but it is also a floating signifier. In this Element, I take a snapshot approach and examine the term at three points in time. In each of them, it refers to something quite different.

The case of new adult therefore poses questions that are larger than the category itself. Indeed, it poses questions about the whole concept of literary categorisation, what it is and how it happens. In this Element, I use new adult fiction as a case study to explore the operations of genre in the contemporary literary marketplace. I push back against notions that a text's genre is something determined (at least, not solely) by the text itself and argue for the importance of paratext as a determining feature (Genette 1997). This encompasses peritext – the material within a volume that is not the text itself, such as cover, spine, blurb, frontmatter and so on – and, perhaps most importantly, epitext, which exists outside the volume. This encompasses readerly spaces such as Goodreads, which, in the case of new adult fiction, proved to be a driving force in the genre's development (see McCracken 2013 for further explication on epitext in the digital literary sphere).

I am informed in my approach to new adult fiction in this Element by the notion of the 'genre world' as theorised by Lisa Fletcher, Beth Driscoll and

Kim Wilkins, which 'describes the collective activity that goes into the creation and circulation of genre texts, and is particularly focused on the communities, collaborations, and industrial pressures that drive and are driven by the processes of socio-artistic formations' (2018, 997). This is a modification of Howard S. Becker's notion of the 'art world', a model which positions art as the product of collective activity, rather than that of a lone artist (2008). Fletcher, Driscoll and Wilkins apply this to the popular fiction publishing industry in the twenty-first century and argue that a genre world is composed of three parts: it is a sector of the publishing industry, a social formation and a body of texts (2018, 997). They observe that much literary studies scholarship focuses on the third of these – the body of texts – to the detriment of the other two (2018, 997). Therefore, I adopt a more holistic approach in this Element, one that takes into account the paratextual and extratextual factors that influence how texts embody genres and how these genres develop. To understand the evolution of new adult fiction – and, more broadly, how genres shift, are shaped and develop in the contemporary literary marketplace – we must also examine the industrial and social forces in play.

The term 'new adult', as far as I have been able to determine, has been applied almost exclusively to books. As such, this is a study of a literary phenomenon, and the methods used herein derive from literary and publishing studies. However, questions of genre and categorisation are relevant well outside the literary sphere, and genres of all kinds are subject to the tripartite influences of industry, social formations and texts themselves. Because of this, it is my hope that the arguments I present in this Element will have relevance not just outside the study of new adult fiction but also outside the study of literature, in the broader study of media and communication.

Category vs Genre

A common claim that circulates about young adult (YA) fiction in popular literary discourse is that it is not a genre. 'YA is not a genre – it is a readership', writes literary agent and author Danielle Binks in an article in the Australian literary journal *Kill Your Darlings*. She argues that YA 'spans the spectrum of fiction genres from mystery to literary fiction, horror and romance', containing within it examples of all these things. The term 'young adult', in this context, refers to the 'proposed age-bracket of the intended readership' (2014). Likewise, Tracy van Straaten, vice president at Scholastic, was quoted in an *Atlantic* article, saying that '[s]omething that people tend to forget is that YA is a category not a genre, and within it is every possible genre: fantasy, sci-fi, contemporary, non-fiction' (Doll 2012). Author Chuck Wendig wrote the following on his blog:

> Young Adult is a proposed *age range* for those who wish to read a particular book. It is a demographic rather than an agglomeration of people who like to read stories about, say, Swashbuckling Dinosaur Princesses or Space Manatee Antiheroes or whatever the cool kid genres are these days. Repeat after me: *Young Adult is not a genre designation*. (2013, emphasis in original)

Some commentators have activist reasons for making this distinction. Binks notes that 'critics and commentators would be less likely to write off an entire *readership*, than they are to criticise a single supposed genre' (2014, emphasis in original), pointing to the way that 'genre' is often seen as a marker of the lowbrow. In an article for the popular literary website Book Riot, Kelly Jensen argues that if YA is referred to 'as a genre, as opposed to category of literature', then it will be 'so easy for teens [i.e. the intended readers] to be pushed out and for adults to feel more ownership' (2019). She goes on to distinguish among 'category', 'genre' and 'mood':

> A category of books, however, is broader than a mood or a genre. A category is who the book is intended for. It's part of the marketing of a book, as well as a way for those who work with books to quickly ascertain the reader for whom the book would be most appropriate. Think of the category as an umbrella, with mood and genre falling beneath it. You have adult books as a category, and beneath it, you have mysteries, thrillers, romance, fantasy, and so forth. You can then weave mood among those genre. (2019)

I am not especially interested in proving these commentators wrong. In many ways, in fact, I would argue that they are correct. Young adult fiction (as well as the earliest incarnations of new adult fiction) is a literary category in a different way from something like romance fiction, crime fiction or fantasy fiction. Writing about children's fiction, Perry Nodelman argues that texts are 'included in this category by virtue of what the category implies, not so much about the text itself as about its intended audience' (2008, 3). These are distinctions we could also apply to more recent and specific marketing category designations, such as middle-grade fiction (targeted towards ages 8–12) and young adult fiction (targeted to teenagers). Hence, we come back to the notion that YA is not a genre, but a category, defined by its intended market rather than any particular features of the texts. Implicit in this is the assumption that 'genre' is defined by features of the text, while 'category' is defined by intended market.

While this distinction between category and genre has its uses, I differ from the previously mentioned commentators in that I do not believe that this distinction is as clear as it might seem on the surface. While YA fiction does not have a specific narrative mandate in terms of plot trajectory, it does have distinguishing textual features: for instance, it would be very unusual to find a book in the category that does not feature teenage protagonists. Similarly, in genres defined by plot trajectory, such as romance fiction, which is defined by its 'central love story' and 'emotionally satisfying and optimistic ending' (RWA, n.d.), the audience is unspoken but implied. This is also true for genres defined by more amorphous, not necessarily plot-based, textual features, such as fantasy, defined largely by the impossibility of its storyworld (Clute 1997). Unless stated otherwise, the presumption is that it is targeted to adults.

Here, I am following Nodelman, who argues, 'children's literature also implies its other: adult literature' (2008, 340). Unless a book explicitly brands itself otherwise – for example, young adult romance – then the assumption is that the intended reader demographic is adults. This does not mean that younger readers will *not* read it (indeed, 'reading up' is a noted phenomenon, as is adult readership of YA and other forms of children's literature); rather, they are not the text's implied market. Therefore, we might also contend that as the young adult romance is defined by both its implied audience and promised plot structure, so too is the more generic romance novel. This is doubly provable when we consider that 'romance' is a genre which falls under the broader umbrella of popular fiction. This is, as Nodelman notes, another descriptor for a certain kind of text that focuses on audience rather than plot (2008, 3).

The distinction between the audience-based 'category' and the plot-based 'genre' is thus at least somewhat fuzzy: a fuzziness that can lead to substantial generic evolution, as we will see over the course of this Element's exploration of new adult fiction. Both forms imply what Frederick Jameson describes as a 'contract' between writer and reader (1975, 135), in that both make a certain kind of promise. This creates what Tzvetan Todorov and Richard M. Berrong call a 'horizon of expectations' for the reader, even if those expectations might focus more heavily on who that reader is than on the nature of the plot (1976, 163).

I also want to push back against this binaristic demarcation of category vs genre by suggesting that in spaces like the physical space of the bookstore or the digital space of a platform like Goodreads, the distinction does not particularly matter. Here, every category/genre is, effectively, a marketing category, whether that category is shaped by implied audience, implied plot trajectory or some other combination of metrics. In this assertion, I am informed strongly by the work of Claire Squires, who argues that publisher taxonomies are 'a form of branding, a way of grouping and hence distinguishing products in the marketplace in order to capitalize on customer experience and perception of products and to maximise their visibility' (2007, 85).

While I am aware of – and agree with, at least in part – the distinctions between category and genre raised by the commentators I have quoted here, I am henceforth going to (perhaps somewhat controversially) use the words 'genre' and 'category' interchangeably in this Element, where I define the former term the way Squires does: '[g]enre, including the genre of literary fiction, is a marketing concept in publishing: a definition not for its own sake but one which has commercial implications' (2007, 5). I do not do so to be polemical but because a neat demarcation of categorisation by plot trajectory vs categorisation by intended audience simply does not hold up in the case of new adult fiction. As the following sections will show, new adult does not fit easily into either of these categories but has bled substantially between the two. This has implications for how we think about categorisation more broadly, as textual features and intended readerships are not as easily distinguishable as they might initially seem.

This discussion of category vs genre is also necessary background to understand some of the vitriol with which people have reacted to new adult fiction. Notably, much of this commentary refers to the mere existence of the category rather than any particular texts that bear the genre label, something that reveals numerous assumptions about the ways we think about literary categorisation.

'"New adult" fiction is now an official literary genre because marketers want us to buy things', read the headline of a 2012 *Jezebel* article by Katie Baker. 'Let's be honest', Baker goes on to argue in the body of the article, '*marketers* need "New Adult" fiction – which really just means books about millennials, right? – to be a stand-alone genre, not readers' (2012, emphasis in original). This is indicative of an opinion that coloured much of the coverage of new adult as a literary category, especially in 2012–13, when it began to penetrate mainstream bestseller lists. Michael Stearns, former editorial director for HarperCollins Children's Books, called 'new adult' a 'breezily condescending handle' with the potential to 'ghettoize' books with twenty-something protagonists (2009). An article by Lauren Sarner in the *Huffington Post* decried it as 'a label that is condescending to readers and authors alike', not because of the quality of texts but because of the assumption that such a label was required at all (2013).

This negative commentary reveals something about how new adult fiction has been perceived: as a literary category created as a cynical marketing ploy to mobilise a particular demographic (people in their twenties). This assumption also demonstrates the assertion from Squires that I quoted at the end of the previous section: genre and marketing are deeply linked in publishing, and the logic of literary categorisation is a commercial logic (2007). Here, the term 'new adult' is assumed to denote a certain market, positioning it alongside young adult fiction, where the implied audience is the primary defining feature. The strong negative reactions expressed by these and other commentators have discrete but intertwined roots in three implied assumptions: (1) that adults in their twenties need books marketed especially to them; (2) that these books will necessarily be more infantile in quality because of the proposed demarcation of audience, as other forms of fiction demarcated by audience are primarily for children (Nodelman 2008, 340); and (3) that this demarcation is plainly for commercial reasons, rather than serving any kind of expressed audience need.

We could also add a fourth point, commonly expressed in another form of commentary on new adult fiction: (4) it is a literary category that does not appear – initially, at least – to be defined by any kind of plot features beyond, perhaps, a protagonist belonging to a certain age bracket. Alongside the negative commentary I have noted, which decried the usefulness of the category, were many that queried – and in some cases lamented – its nebulousness, with oft-repeated titles like 'What Is New Adult Fiction?' 'What's New about New Adult?' and 'Is "New Adult" Fiction Going to Be a Thing?' (Brookover, Burns & Jensen 2013; Engberg 2014; Gold 2016; Hoffman 2010; Kieffer 2017; Smith 2012; Wetta 2013). '[T]he consensus on New Adult is that there is no consensus', one librarian wrote (Gomez 2013). Inherent in this assumption is the notion that a literary category *should* be defined by textual features, as the romance genre is shaped by its central love story and happy ending, or fantasy is defined by the presence of the fantastic, but that these features have not been identified. This leaves our other metric for defining a category – the implied readership – which, as seen earlier, was not received warmly by some.

Despite this, the term 'new adult fiction' has persisted. Since its first appearance in mainstream literary discourse in 2009, the term has continued to denote a certain kind of fiction. Many attempts have been made to define it, based on features including, but not limited to, theme, narrative voice, protagonist age, readership age and the diegetic inclusion of sex (Brookover, Burns & Jensen 2013; Carmack 2012; Jae 2014; Pattinson 2014; West 2014; Wetta 2013). However, as I mentioned at the beginning of this Introduction, as I have argued briefly elsewhere (McAlister 2018a, 2018b), and as I will argue in more depth over the course of this Element, what 'new adult' denotes has evolved substantially. This means that a single, fixed definition cannot encompass the term, and to attempt to provide one would not only do a disservice to the category but also would fail to recognise the complex and changing ways that genres emerge and develop in the contemporary literary marketplace.

This is the central argument of this Element. Using new adult fiction as a case study and tracing how it has developed since its inception in 2009, my goal here is to demonstrate the fluidity and porousness of literary genres in the contemporary market. In particular, I seek to demonstrate that the boundaries between categories demarcated primarily by implied audience and those demarcated primarily by textual features are not as firm as it might initially seem by tracing how new adult fiction evolved from being a satellite category of young adult fiction to becoming a sub-genre of romance fiction. In doing so, I aim to demonstrate that paratextual features have a huge influence in shaping genre identities and understandings; that marketing plays a fundamental role in literary taxonomies; and that in the world of popular fiction, 'genre' and 'marketing category' are functionally the same thing.

About This Element

As discussed earlier, what the term 'new adult' means has changed enormously over the decade or so of its existence, and so to provide a single definition of it would be fraught. Here, I follow Kim Wilkins, who asserts that 'genres are not static, ahistorical categories. Rather, genres are processes. They are formed, negotiated and reformed, both tacitly and explicitly, by the interactions of authors, readers and (importantly) institutions' (2005). To account for this, I am taking a snapshot approach to investigating new adult fiction (McAlister 2018a), providing an overview of it at three distinct periods of time to map its generic development. The first section of this Element focuses on the beginning of new adult fiction at St Martin's Press in 2009. The second section examines the new adult boom period of 2011–13, focusing particularly on how the term 'new adult' was co-opted by readerly and writerly communities in digital fora like Goodreads. Finally, the third section interrogates the texts currently marketed and sold as new adult at the time of writing in 2020, so as to consider where this particular category has ended up, about a decade since its inception.

Taking into account Fletcher, Driscoll and Wilkins' assertion that the textual is often privileged at the expense of the industrial and social in studies of genre (2018), I have chosen to focus on the latter two rather than the former. The industrial and social spheres are where much of the paratextual – especially epitextual – work of genre is done, and my goal in this Element is to show how fundamental these areas are to any interrogation of how genre operates. There is, therefore, little close reading in this Element. Indeed, to attempt close reading of any kind of representative corpus of new adult texts would be a fraught process, not least in determining what 'representative' might mean, as any kind of selection process runs the risk of imposing artificial inclusion and exclusion criteria that do not sufficiently capture how genre works in practice.

However, it is not possible – or desirable – to take the textual dimension out altogether. While I focus more on the paratextual than the textual in this Element, peritexts and epitexts cannot exist independently of texts, and it is not possible to study them and the role they play in the operations of genre without positioning them in relation to texts. Nor would it be good scholarly practice to attempt to give an account of a genre's history without being very well-read in that genre. Rather than close reading, my engagement with the textual sphere of new adult fiction in this Element draws more on distant reading as theorised by Franco Moretti (2005, 2013), which allows for patterns to be identified across a corpus by stepping back from the texts. Here, distance is 'not an obstacle, but a *specific form of knowledge*: fewer elements, hence a sharper sense of their overall interconnection' (2005, 1, emphasis in original). Specifically, my reading of the texts categorised as new adult by industrial and/or social forces was to examine how well they mapped onto understandings of other genres – in particular, YA and romance, to which new adult has been akin at various points in its evolution.

1 2009 – New Adult at St Martin's Press

In his book *Genre*, John Frow contends the following:

> In thinking about genre as a process it becomes important to
> think about the conditions that sustain it: the institutional
> forces that govern the determination and distribution of
> classification and value. Genres emerge and survive because
> they meet a demand, because they can be materially sup-
> ported, because there are readers and appropriate conditions
> of reading (literacy, affordable texts), writers or producers
> with the means to generate those texts, and institutions to
> circulate and channel them. (2014, 210)

To summarise this somewhat: many of the factors that determine whether
a genre will emerge, whether it will survive and whether it will thrive are
paratextual and extratextual, not textual. The existence of the texts is not
enough. A potential readership must exist, and a body of authors must exist
capable of catering to this readership: readerly and writerly communities that
fall under the 'social formation' sector of the publishing world as theorised by
Fletcher, Driscoll & Wilkins (2018). Moreover, institutional and industrial
forces must be able to connect the readers and the writers, supporting the
growth of the genre and assisting the texts to find their market.

Frow's contentions around why genres emerge and how they survive are
a useful way to trace the origins and initial failure of new adult fiction. The
existence of texts that could be classified under the new adult label was, in
a lot of ways, somewhat irrelevant. The term was coined to mobilise
a particular *readership*. Moreover, it was not texts that stalled the progress
of the new adult category. Rather, it was institutional forces and factors that
existed outside the domain of the textual.

1.1 Post-Adolescence: St Martin's Press and the New Adult Submissions Contest

As I have written elsewhere, '[t]he origins of the genre category "new
adult" are artificial, not organic: it was made, not born' (McAlister 2018a, 4).

The term 'new adult' was coined in 2009 in a submissions contest from St Martin's Press, in which they were

> actively looking for great, new, cutting edge fiction with protagonists who are slightly older than YA and can appeal to an adult audience. Since twenty-somethings are devouring YA, St. Martin's Press is seeking fiction similar to YA that can be published and marketed as adult – a sort of 'older YA' or 'new adult'. (Jae-Jones 2009a)

If we return to Frow, we can see here the first factor he lists that determines a genre's emergence and survival: 'meet[ing] a demand' (2014, 210). As discussed in the Introduction, YA fiction is a literary category defined primarily by its intended readership, rather than by specific plot elements or structures. The implied reader of the YA text – in both senses of the term as outlined by Wolf Schmid, that is, as 'presumed addressee' and 'ideal recipient' (2013) – is a teenager. In this call for submissions, however, St Martin's has noted the demand for YA in a different demographic: 'twenty-somethings' (Jae-Jones 2009a). The logic inherent here is clear: YA is currently fulfilling a need for these readers, and if St Martin's can create a new category that positions this demographic as the presumed addressees and ideal recipients, then it can more precisely exploit this market, as well as potentially adding a new tranche of sales on top of the existing sales of YA it was already making to that demographic. It was attempting to 'popularise literature through labelling', which Nicci Gerrard (1989, 118) notes is a key feature of genre publishing, as well as 'market-making', which John Thompson (2012, 30–1) contends is the hallmark of a good publisher.

The mind behind the concept of new adult was Dan Weiss, who was hired by St Martin's as publisher-at-large for the purposes of creating content for 'twenty-somethings, Gen Yers, and older young adult readers – those emerging adults who are navigating career, love and family in a 24/7 connected world' (Publisher's Marketplace, quoted in McBride 2009a). Weiss had previously worked as an editor for Golden Books and Scholastic, but he was best known as a book packager, particularly of series fiction for young adults. After beginning his career as a comic book editor and spending some time running Scholastic's Teen Age Book Club in the late 1970s, he began his own book packaging company in the 1980s (Andriani 2009; Kephart 2012; Mead 2009). In conjunction with the mass-market paperback imprint Bantam, he began publishing the *Sweet Dreams* series of category romance novels targeted at the teenage market. These were 'essentially, Harlequin romances for kids' (Mead 2009) and followed the model of category romance publishing pioneered by Harlequin Mills & Boon and adopted in North America by imprints like Silhouette: defined first by publisher and then by thematically determined line (Fletcher & McAlister 2019). A few years later, Weiss and Bantam innovated by beginning the *Sweet Valley High* teen romance series, which used a more soap operatic style and was defined by common recurring characters in a single world rather than purely by paratextual imprint/line branding, credited to a single author – Francine Pascal (Pattee 2011, 21). This model proved to be successful and replicable, and Weiss' company was also responsible for numerous other highly successful mass-market series targeted at young adults, including *The Vampire Diaries* in the 1990s and, after its acquisition by Alloy Entertainment in 2000, *Gossip Girl*, *Pretty Little Liars* and *The Sisterhood of the Travelling Pants* (Andriani 2009; Kephart 2012; Mead 2009).

This was not Weiss' only experience in creating and marketing content specifically to young people. In the 2000s, prior to taking up his position as publisher-at-large at St Martin's, he spent eight years as the publisher and managing director of SparkNotes, a popular purveyor of online study guides, which Weiss reportedly saw as a 'logical extension of [his] years publishing for teens' (Kephart 2012; see also Andriani 2009; Halverson 2014). Certainly, it was a logical extension in terms of packaging and branding material for high school and college-aged students: as literary agent Kristin Nelson remarked when Weiss took up his new position at St Martin's, 'Dan has been in the biz for a good long time and he particularly knows publishing for young people' (2009).

Weiss appears to have believed in the possibility of an older market for fiction targeted at young adults since his days as a book packager. In the 1990s, his company developed the *Fearless* series in conjunction with *Sweet*

Valley High's Francine Pascal, in which the seventeen-year-old protagonist ran 'through a gauntlet of violence, romance, philosophy and solitude' (Halverson 2014, 22). Apparently, Weiss agitated publisher Simon & Schuster to market the *Fearless* series to an adult audience. Simon & Schuster refused the request, but Weiss purportedly 'saw that as the beginning of what he knew would be a new kind of publishing, one he would eventually dub New Adult fiction' (Halverson 2014, 22). According to his assistant S. Jae-Jones, Weiss believed that

> the market for young adults – that is, adults who are young – is largely untapped. We are a generation that grew up reading YA, but once we grew up, we couldn't find fiction in the adult sections applicable to our lives.... We're looking for books that call to us (Dan calls us 'Gen Y') and there is a lot in YA that is appealing: finding a place in life, discovering who we are, etc. Hence we [St Martin's] want to find books that are like YA, but targeted to us slightly older readers. McBride 2009b

Given Weiss' areas of expertise, it is not surprising that new adult was framed in marketing terms in this early stage of its development. This is evident not just in the initial call for contest submissions, which explicitly asked for 'fiction similar to YA that can be published and marketed as adult' (Jae-Jones 2009a), but in the way Weiss and St Martin's sought to give a name to the demographic. In the previous quote, we see them referred to as 'Gen Y' (McBride 2009b). In the call for contest submissions, they are addressed as 'twenty-somethings' (Jae-Jones 2009a). Both these terms are used in the announcement of Weiss' hire, alongside the term 'emerging adults' (Publisher's Marketplace, quoted in McBride 2009a). This is also the term used by children's literature and library science scholar Amy Pattee when she defines new adult fiction as 'a literary category dependent on a relationship between the books in this category and a particular audience that has been constructed, of late, as "emerging adults"' (2017, 219). Here, Pattee draws on psychologist Jeffrey Jensen Arnett's theorisation of emerging adulthood: he contends that 'common changes have taken place with respect to the lives of young people . . . a new period of the life course has been developed between adolescence and young adulthood' (2000, 69–70). This makes emerging adulthood a liminal space between the two states: a space where they 'have reached their majority and enjoy the rights and privileges associated with this milestone; furthermore, they form peer communities in and around institutions of postsecondary education and engage in serious romantic relationships' (Pattee 2017, 220). Notably, Weiss openly admitted that he and St Martin's were trying to coin the term 'new adult' not just as a name for a literary category but also for the demographic: '[w]e're trying to coin the phrase "new adults", and we'd like to see more of it', Weiss said in an interview, 'I think it's an overlooked category' (PT Editors 2010).

Essentially, what Weiss and St Martin's were attempting to do was to name the market – the ideal reader and presumed addressee (Schmid 2013) – and thus reverse engineer the literary category. If we use Frow's terms: St Martin's sought to name the reader, position itself as the institution with the means to circulate and channel the texts for these readers and thus satisfy (or, more cynically, provoke) a demand (2014, 210). Notably, St Martin's also provided an example of what this reader might look like. The face of the call for contest submissions was not Weiss but rather his editorial assistant S. 'JJ' Jae-Jones.[1] Nearly all communication about the contest flowed from Jae-Jones. The call for entries was not hosted on any official St Martin's platform but, instead, on her blog *Uncreated Conscience* (2009a). The announcement of the winners also appeared on Jae-Jones' blog, and almost all information about what St Martin's was looking for in the contest flowed from her. She frequently positioned herself as part of the demographic St Martin's was trying to formalise through naming. For example:

> But what about 'postadolescent' fiction? That's a bit harder
> to articulate. We, the 'new adults', have some perspective on
> our lives, but scope? We're not old enough, we're not

[1] Jae-Jones is now the author of two *New York Times* bestselling novels, *Wintersong* and *Shadowsong*, which are frequently shelved as new adult on Goodreads.

> experienced enough, we're simply not grown-up enough.
> Our lives have immediacy, just as a teenager's does, but we
> also possess the wisdom to understand that this immediacy
> cannot last for long. It's a curious place in life and Dan
> [Weiss] and I feel that not enough fiction (or nonfiction)
> explore this nebulous time of life. The 'quarter-life crisis', if
> you will. (Jae-Jones 2009b)

This rhetorical manoeuvre is likewise evident in the excerpt I quoted earlier from Jae-Jones' interview on Georgia McBride's blog, where she firmly positions herself as one of the potential readers for new adult: 'we want to find books that are like YA, but targeted to *us slightly older readers*' (McBride 2009b, my emphasis).

McBride was also a key figure in St Martin's attempt to propagate the concept of new adult. The submissions contest was sponsored by #YALitChat, a weekly Twitter chat founded and hosted by McBride for people involved or aspiring to be involved in any aspect of YA, and McBride and Jae-Jones were the two readers for submissions (Jae-Jones 2009a; McBride 2009c). The association with McBride and #YALitChat reinforced the strong association between young adult and new adult, a further example of how St Martin's was seeking to mobilise the existing post-teen readership of the former. This is also evident in the term 'new adult' itself, which is not especially legible without reference to 'young adult'. The term both drew borders between the two categories in terms of implied readership and emphasised their common ground.

By utilising Jae-Jones as a figurehead for the contest and an example of the implied readership, St Martin's also functionally highlighted the common ground for new adult and adult fiction, while drawing borders between them. Jae-Jones was clearly an adult – she was a professional with an aspirational job working for a well-known publisher – but she was also, as shown earlier, positioned rhetorically as 'simply not grown-up enough' to be a 'true' adult (Jae-Jones 2009b). In her own words (note again the rhetorical manoeuvre in which Jae-Jones positions herself as part of the target readership): 'We might have jobs, marriages, and some even mortgages (lucky bastards), but we still haven't settled into our adult skins. I still think of myself as a 'girl' too – I'm 24, engaged, and I've been a 'responsible' adult for over 4 years now, but somehow I still feel like a fraud' (Jae-Jones 2009c).

Jae-Jones positioned the ideal reader of new adult as an adult, rather than the teen reader of YA: when asked where new adult should be shelved, her response was '[o]n the adult shelves' (2009c). However, she was frank about the commercial reasons behind St Martin's attempt to coin the new term. 'I will be straight – adult fiction is flailing,' she wrote. 'Are publishers ... looking to tap into YA's popularity? Of course' (2009c). But she also clearly sought to articulate that this liminal adult-but-not-adult demographic existed, and only a paucity of fiction served them, especially in the adult section of a bookstore:

> Do I find great fiction in the adult sections of the store? Absolutely. But it's harder – I have to wade through [a lot] that doesn't interest me: divorces, having a family, affairs, mid-life crises. I'm closer in age and in place in life to teens than I am to someone who is 35. (Jae-Jones 2009c)

Jae-Jones provided a list of adult titles she asserted could have been published as new adult, which encompassed literary fiction (*The Brief Wondrous Life of Oscar Wao* by Junot Diaz, *Kafka on the Shore* by Haruki Murakami), creative non-fiction (*A Heartbreaking Work of Staggering Genius* by Dave Eggers), crime fiction (*The Girl with the Dragon Tattoo* by Stieg Larsson), historical fiction (*The Girl with the Pearl Earring* by Tracey Chevalier, *Memoirs of a Geisha* by Arthur Golden), fantasy (*Neverwhere* by Neil Gaiman, the *Kushiel's Legacy* series by Jacqueline Carey), paranormal romance (the *Night Huntress* series by Jeanine Frost) and chick lit (*The Devil Wears Prada* by Lauren Weisberger, *The Nanny Diaries* by Emma McLaughlin and Nicola Kraus). She also provided a list of young adult titles that she asserted could have been published as new adult, including Malinda Lo's queer Cinderella retelling *Ash*, Kristin Cashore's romantic fantasy *Graceling*, E. Lockhart's boarding school novel *The Disreputable History of Frankie Landau-Banks* and Marcus Zusak's

Holocaust novel *The Book Thief* (2009c). There is a substantial amount of generic diversity across these titles: it was clear that this imagined version of new adult fiction did not come with a mandated plot trajectory. Rather, its sole defining textual feature was a protagonist or protagonists who fit in this 'twenty-something'/'Gen Y'/'emerging adult' post-adolescent demographic – a protagonist who mirrored the readership St Martin's sought to court.

While, as noted, Jae-Jones recommended that new adult books be shelved for the meantime with adult books, she also commented that St Martin's eventual hope was that the category would grow large enough that it would receive its own shelf space in bookstores, much as children's literature was split into picture book, middle grade and young adult spaces (2009c). This, I contend, was at the heart of a great deal of the negative reaction to new adult, which, as I noted in the Introduction to this Element, was rooted in three implied assumptions: (1) adults in their twenties need books marketed especially to them, (2) this proposed demarcation in audience means that the books will be more infantile and (3) this demarcation is purely commercial. Although St Martin's sought to draw young adult/new adult and new adult/adult borders and children's literature is one of the few types of fiction categorised by presumed audience rather than by narrative content, we can see here how this push to separate new adult from adult fiction might be read as infantilising an already adult readership (Nodelman 2008).

1.2 Contest, Context: The Texts and What Happened Next

St Martin's is regularly credited with being the progenitor of new adult fiction. This is not untrue, given how Weiss and Jae-Jones created and mobilised the term, as outlined earlier. However, the actual texts are regularly disappeared from the discussion: something that has greatly impacted the ways in which new adult is discussed and understood, including in some of the scant extant scholarship on the genre (cf. Pattee 2017).

The hiring of a high-profile executive like Dan Weiss with substantial experience in creating and sustaining literary brands makes it seem like St Martin's put a great deal of effort into developing the term 'new adult' as a descriptor for both a readership and a literary category. However, it is worth noting firstly that the contest was publicised extremely early in Weiss' tenure at St Martin's, which implies that it was more experimental than part of a long-term deliberate strategy. Likewise, there is not much other evidence to suggest that St Martin's was heavily invested in the contest. While the new adult concept seems to have come from Weiss – unsurprising, given his expertise in branding – the majority of the work appears to have been done by his assistant Jae-Jones: '[Weiss] has rather benignly given me complete independence with this project,' she told McBride (2009d). Although there were some labour costs, these were perhaps unanticipated: according to Jae-Jones, she and Weiss planned to respond to every submission they received (McBride 2009b), and they did not expect to receive as many as they did, which was 382 – Jae-Jones apparently hoped to receive 50 (McBride 2009d). While it might have been 'simply unheard of for a large publisher to read and vet that many submissions in such a short period of time' (McBride 2009d), the submissions received were short: two-to-three–line pitches and first paragraphs (McBride 2009c). The prizes for the competition were similarly small. Each of three winners received a copy of *Tempted* by P. C. and Kristin Cast (two of St Martin's most popular YA authors). These three winners, along with another fifteen entrants (i.e. 18 submissions out of the 382 received), were asked to submit a one-to-two-page synopsis and the first fifty pages of their manuscript to St Martin's (Jae-Jones 2009d; McBride 2009d).

A brief overview of the eighteen submissions that proceeded to the next step with St Martin's can be seen in Table 1.

While I should note that the accuracy of Table 1 is dependent entirely on my own research abilities, and it is possible that some books were so dramatically revised and retitled that I could not find them in my search, one thing is clear: none of the competition winners were ultimately published by St Martin's. In a post-competition interview, McBride asked Jae-Jones when the next competition would be – 'some are already asking when the next contest will be. So???' – but Jae-Jones only replied, '[i]f we find something from this one, maybe Boss [Weiss] will be open to another

Table 1 St Martin's contest winners (Jae-Jones 2009d; McBride 2009e)

Title	Author	Brief Description	Genre	Later Published?
Vinnie's Diner	Al Lee, Jennifer	Heroine finds herself in a purgatorial diner after dying in a car accident.	Fantasy	Yes (traditional, Abingdon, UK)
Untitled novel about hipster/ working stiff	Barkley, Simon	Two souls end up in one man's body and have to battle for supremacy.	Fantasy	No
Untitled novel with obituary writer	Beattie, Nicole	Obituary writer gets followed home from haunted house by succubus.	Fantasy	Yes, as *Poe* by J Lincoln Fenn (traditional, 47North)
A Mad, Wicked Folly	Biggs [Waller], Sharon	Edwardian heroine runs away from family to join suffragettes.	Historical	Yes (traditional, Viking)
Party Like It's 1899	Brice, Amanda	College junior time-travels to 1899 Paris.	Fantasy	No (self-publication apparently planned but does not seem to have occurred)

Table 1 Cont.

Title	Author	Brief Description	Genre	Later Published?
Untitled Princess Elisa novel	Carson, Rae	Underachiever princess has to save the world.	Fantasy	Yes, as *The Girl of Fire and Thorns* (traditional, Green Willow)
After the End	Davidson, Bonnie	American dystopia, set immediately after a zombie apocalypse.	Science fiction (dystopia)	Yes (self-published under name Bonnie Dee)
Picture of Fate	Diamond, Laura	College freshman has to protect her vampire boyfriend's secret.	Fantasy	No
The Art of Carving Mettle	Hacha, Barbara	Heroine learns to survive as depression-era train hobo.	Historical	Yes, self-published as *Line by Line*
Twenty-Somewhere (contest winner)	Hoffman, Kristan	Episodic narratives following three best friends.	Contemporary	Yes (self-published as a compendium post-competition; published to the web before competition)

Title	Author	Description	Genre	Published?
The Dharma Bum Business (contest winner)	Hoole, Elissa	F/F roadtrip romance.	Contemporary	Yes, as *Kiss the Morning Star* (traditional, Marshall Cavendish)
The World and Its Parts	Johnston, Glenn P.	Down on his luck hero falls in love with a girl with secrets.	Contemporary	No
May Queen	Long, Ruth F.	Heroine has to rescue her brother from fairy realm.	Fantasy	Yes, as *The Treachery of Beautiful Things* (traditional, Dial Books)
Zombie Proof Fence (contest winner)	Morehead, M. P.	Australian dystopia, set three years after a zombie apocalypse.	Science fiction (dystopia)	No
Mall Bats	Pab [no surname]	Manager of a mall music store is transformed into a vampire.	Fantasy	No
Waiting	Rummel, Jennifer	Heroine searches for identity in her first year of college.	Contemporary (verse novel)	No

Table 1 Cont.

Title	Author	Brief Description	Genre	Later Published?
Bernardo the Daredevil	Tennis, Luke	Son narrates his father's midlife crisis.	Contemporary	No, but previously self-published prior to the competition
Vertere	Winn, Topie	Protagonist moves to New York and meets the people who will change his life forever.	Contemporary	Yes (self-published)

one' (McBride 2009d). Weiss, it seems, was as good as his word: the contest did not result in any new books for St Martin's, and so no further contests were held.

This is not to say that the concept of new adult was dead in the water at St Martin's. In early 2011, Jae-Jones published a blog post outlining the acquisitions they had made for 'our New Adult endeavour' (2011). These appear in Table 2.

St Martin's were clearly courting the twenty-something audience with these books. However, while Zelevansky and Burgess used the term 'new adult' in blog interviews about their novels (Anderson 2012; Moore 2012), St Martin's only used it in reference to Francine Pascal's *Sweet Valley Confidential*. Even then, it is used in a way imbued with curious ambiguity. The marketing blurb describes the book as a 'striking new adult novel from author and creator Francine Pascal' (Macmillan n.d.), which can be read in multiple ways – as a 'new adult' novel or as a new 'adult novel' from an author historically known for the teen-targeted *Sweet Valley High* series.

In short: the term 'new adult' certainly made waves when the contest was announced in late 2009, and it had a long enough life that authors like Zelevansky and Burgess could mobilise it in interviews for their 2012 releases (although this might be tied to the new adult boom period, discussed in Section 2, rather than the original iteration of the term). However, there is not much evidence to suggest that St Martin's invested heavily in the term itself. While the press clearly continued to pursue the twenty-something demographic, by the time Weiss resigned in 2013, St Martin's had no specifically branded new adult lines, imprints, or properties.

1.3 Context, Paratext: New Adult and Genre in 2009

In Table 1, I gave a brief description of each of the eighteen titles shortlisted in the St Martin's competition, and a broad generic categorisation. Notably, there was some generic diversity in the titles: six contemporary (including one verse novel), eight fantasy, two historical, and two science fiction (both zombie dystopias). Table 1 also showed that several of these books were published, some traditionally and some independently. Table 3 shows the top three Goodreads genre categories under which

Table 2 St Martin's new adult acquisitions as of January 2011 (Jae-Jones 2011)

Title	Author	Brief Description	Genre
Union Street [published as *Brooklyn Girls*]	Burgess, Gemma	First in a series about friends living in Brooklyn.	Fiction (contemporary)
Dating in the Nude [published as *Getting Naked*]	Cohen, Harlan	Dating advice book.	Non-fiction
Working Girl: How to Have a Fabulous Life on 30 Grand [published as *Quickiechick's Cheat Sheet to Life, Love, Food, Fitness, Fashion, and Finance on a Less Than Fabulous Budget*]	House, Laurel	How-to guide for young women.	Non-fiction
Sweet Valley Confidential	Pascal, Francine	Return to Sweet Valley High characters ten years later.	Fiction (contemporary)
The Roaring Twenties: Adulthood Redefined [published as *Mission Adulthood*]	Seligson, Hannah	Semi-memoir, meditation on adulthood.	Non-fiction

Deal of the Century [published as *Groupon's Biggest Deal Ever*]	Sennett, Frank	Account of the rise of Groupon.	Non-fiction
The Pfeffernoose Chronicles [published as *Semi-Charmed Life*]	Zelevansky, Nora	A young woman starts writing a blog for a glamourous New York socialite.	Fiction (contemporary)

Table 3 Goodreads shelves for published contest finalists

Title	Author	Goodreads Shelf #1	Goodreads Shelf #2	Goodreads Shelf #3
Vinnie's Diner	Al Lee, Jennifer	Fiction	Religion	
Poe [Untitled novel with obituary writer]	Fenn, J Lincoln [Beattie, Nicole]	Horror	Fantasy	Fantasy > Paranormal
A Mad, Wicked Folly	Biggs [Waller], Sharon	Historical > Historical fiction	Young Adult	Historical
Girl of Fire and Thorns [Untitled Princess Elisa novel]	Carson, Rae	Fantasy	Young Adult	Romance
After the End	Dee, Bonnie [Davidson, Bonnie]	Horror > zombies	Horror	Science fiction > apocalyptic
Line by Line [*The Art of Carving Mettle*]	Hacha, Barbara	Fiction	Historical > Historical fiction	

Twenty-Somewhere	Hoffman, Kristan	Women's fiction > chick lit	New adult	Fiction
Kiss the Morning Star [*The Dharma Bum Business*]	Hoole, Elissa	Young adult	Contemporary	LGBT
The Treachery of Beautiful Things [*May Queen*]	Long, Ruth F	Fantasy	Young adult	Romance
Vertere	Winn, Topie	[no labels]		

readers shelved the books that were published (where available – some books were not shelved frequently enough to appear on three shelves).[2]

As the table shows, the shortlisted entries were shelved under a variety of genre labels. However, what is most notable is that the label 'new adult' appears in the top three shelves for only one of them: Kristan Hoffman's self-published *Twenty-Somewhere,* which explicitly advertises that it was one of the three winners of the contest in the first line of its Amazon description. If we examine the books that enjoyed the most success – *Girl of Fire and Thorns* by Rae Carson, *A Mad Wicked Folly* by Sharon Biggs Waller and *The Treachery of Beautiful Things* by Ruth F. Long, all traditionally published and shelved hundreds of times on Goodreads, suggesting a reasonably broad distribution and readership – we find the 'new adult' shelf label is noticeably absent even if we examine the ways the books were categorised beyond the top three most-utilised genre shelves. *Girl of Fire and Thorns* was shelved as new adult by five people (while 4,763 shelved it as fantasy, 2,362 as young adult, and 536 as romance). *A Mad Wicked Folly* was shelved as new adult by four people (while 504 shelved it as historical > historical fiction, 300 as young adult, and 171 as historical). *The Treachery of Beautiful Things* was shelved as fantasy by 389 people, young adult by 245 people, and romance by 113 people; at the time of writing, it had never once been shelved as new adult.

We could read this in several ways. The first is simply that the term 'new adult' fell out of use. However, as the next section of this Element will show, this is not the case. The second is that because new adult did not meet with particular levels of approbation from other industry forces, the books were rewritten to fulfil the requirements of other markets, such as young adult. While this is certainly a contributing factor, especially where books were traditionally published, to claim that every single one of the books was dramatically rewritten is hyperbolic and unrealistic. The third – and, in my opinion, most compelling – reading is that what 'new adult' denoted shifted so substantially that many of these competition winners did not fall within its scope.

[2] Goodreads is a key space in which readers identify and shape genre. I will explore Goodreads shelving practices in more detail in Section 2.

We can see evidence of this shift if we look at St Martin's fiction acquisitions in Table 2. While its competition winners spanned several genres of fiction, its fiction acquisitions did not: all three were contemporary. Table 4 provides more detail on the ways in which they were shelved in Goodreads:

The label 'new adult' is the second most frequently used genre shelf for *Brooklyn Girls*. While it falls outside the top three for the other two books, it is tied for the fourth most frequently used genre shelf label for *Semi-Charmed Life*. Only two people shelved *Sweet Valley Confidential* as new adult, but this might be at least partially because of its association with the firmly teen-oriented *Sweet Valley High* franchise. The use of the new adult shelf, though, is not the most interesting thing about this table. Rather, it is the fact that these three books all fit within a quite specific generic category, denoted by the shelf label women's fiction > chick lit.

In the initial competition, St Martin's was quite clear that what it was looking for was generically diverse. Jae-Jones notes this generic diversity as a feature of young adult, and something St Martin's would seek to emulate with new adult: 'One of the things I love about YA is that all of the genres are shelved together: contemporary, science fiction, fantasy, romance, etc. and I hope that one day this will happen for us as well' (2009c). Like YA, the initial vision of new adult was that it would be a generic melting pot, defined by the target demographic of its twenty-something audience, with its only distinguishing textual feature being the age of the protagonist.

Notably, St Martin's resisted the notion that new adult would be analogous with chick lit: indeed, Jae-Jones published a blog post in December 2009 entitled 'New Adult Is Not Necessarily Chick Lit'. 'I won't deny that New Adult will absolutely encompass what is known as "chick lit"', she wrote, 'but to say that will *only* encompass chick lit is too narrow' (2009e, emphasis in original). Nonetheless, the books St Martin's actually acquired – especially *Brooklyn Girls* and *Semi-Charmed Life* – could easily have been published and marketed as chick lit, and no doubt would have been if their acquisition had taken place earlier in the 2000s. As the next section will show, despite St Martin's original vision of new adult as a generic melting pot defined only by its target demographic, the category

Table 4 Goodreads shelves for St Martin's new adult fiction acquisitions

Title	Author	Goodreads Shelf #1	Goodreads Shelf #2	Goodreads Shelf #3
Brooklyn Girls [originally *Union Street*]	Burgess, Gemma	Women's fiction > chick lit	New adult	Contemporary
Sweet Valley Confidential	Pascal, Francine	Women's fiction > chick lit	Young adult	Fiction
Semi-Charmed Life [originally *The Pfeffernoose Chronicles*]	Zelevansky, Nora	Fiction	Women's fiction > chick lit	Contemporary

that emerged in the following few years – and encompassed many of the books published by it – was in reality one that had distinct plot-based generic markers, many of which it shared with chick lit: to the extent that in 2013, literary agent Kristin Nelson published an article entitled 'New Adult – Perhaps the Latest Word for Chick Lit'.

To end this section, I want to return to the words from Frow I quoted at the beginning. Frow argues that the emergence and survival of genres depends on demand, material support, readers and appropriate conditions of reading, writers and producers of texts, and institutions that circulate and channel them (2014, 210). In 2009, the version of new adult fiction that St Martin's was soliciting had many of these factors in play. The number of competition entries suggests that there was no shortage of writers and producers, and the interest generated suggests that there was demand among the readership. The St Martin's endorsement of the competition – and, indeed, the hiring of an executive like Weiss with expertise in targeting this demographic – suggests that there was institutional backing. So what went wrong?

There is likely a plethora of reasons for the initial failure of new adult, but the most obvious one seems to be a lack of buy-in from retail booksellers. While the contest was ongoing, Jae-Jones stated, '[a]lways, always, always publishers need to figure out where buyers at bookstores will place the book, how it will be reviewed, how it will be physically SEEN by potential readers/buyers etc.' (Meadows 2009, emphasis in original). St Martin's did not know whether new adult would have enough momentum to have its own dedicated shelf space – that was 'largely up to the booksellers' – but it was hoping it would (Jae-Jones 2009c). However, while new adult certainly had some momentum online generated by the competition, this did not ultimately seem to extend to retailers. Deborah Halverson claims, following an interview with Weiss, that the key reason this 2009 iteration of new adult did not succeed was indeed to do with physical shelving: retailers were either not interested in creating a new physical shelving space or did not know where to shelve books with the new adult genre label (2014, 23; see also Naughton 2014, 20).

This lack of interest from booksellers is likely a large part of why St Martin's continued to pursue the demographic but not necessarily the term 'new adult'. Where a book is shelved is a key epitextual feature that affects the way we read it, because genre, by its nature, encodes within it expectations. If I pick up a book from the romance section and find that it is in fact a crime novel with no love plot, I am likely to be disappointed, even if it is an excellent crime novel, because it has not filled the generic contract between writer and reader (Jameson 1975). Claire Squires claims that 'genre ... is a crucial component in the marketplace, as it is one of the primary means by which authors and readers communicate' (2007, 70). This is very true, but we should not forget that institutions are a key intermediary in determining how this communication takes place, because major parts of the paratextual work of genre are conducted and constructed by institutions – including, pertinently for new adult fiction, retail booksellers.

As discussed in this section, the version of new adult that St Martin's envisioned did not have plot-based generic markers beyond the age of the protagonist. Instead, like YA, it would encompass many different genres. But even though YA operates generically in a different way to a plot-based genre like crime or romance, the way its readers find it in a physical bookstore is the same: they can simply go to that section of the store. If there is no new adult shelf space, even if there are many authors of new adult fiction and there is demand for these texts from a readership, how is the work of these authors to find the hands of these readers? If we follow Frow and conceive of genre as a process (2014; see also Wilkins 2005), then we can see here the ways in which institutional and industrial forces can stall a genre's emergence, even if both authorships and readerships exist. These forces operate at the paratextual and extratextual level, demonstrating clearly the role that factors outside the text play in the process of genre.

2 2011–2013 – The New Adult Boom

In the preface to the second edition of his book *Merchants of Culture*, John Thompson remarks:

> Writing about a present-day industry is always going to be like shooting at a moving target: no sooner have you finished the text than your subject matter has changed – things happen, events move on and the industry you had captured at a particular point in time now looks slightly different. Immediate obsolescence is the fate that awaits every chronicler of the present. (2012, xi)

Thompson is writing (accurately) about the entirety of the publishing industry here, an institution that is constantly 'in the throes of tumultuous change, struggling to cope with the impact of a technological revolution that is stripping away some of the old certainties, undermining traditional models and opening up new possibilities in ways that are at once exciting and disorientating' (2012, xi). We can see these forces cast in especially sharp relief if we consider the publishing of popular and genre fiction. On the one hand, genre fiction seems to offer a kind of certainty – there are certain key fixed aspects which categorise, for example, romance fiction (plot trajectory) and young adult fiction (protagonist age and target demographic). On the other, the market is so large that it is in a perpetual state of flux, as institutional forces seek to find the next big thing. This ensures that genre operates not as something static but as a process (Frow 2014; Wilkins 2005), constantly adapting and evolving to fit the new state of affairs. This means that projects of genre definition can be deeply fraught.

New adult fiction is an excellent – and particularly pronounced – example of this phenomenon. We saw in the previous section the way that St Martin's sought to build a market for a new kind of book (Thompson 2012, 30–1) by developing the term 'new adult', seeking submissions, and generating interest from potential readerships. However, its efforts were stymied, largely because of other institutional forces, such as retail booksellers, which would not provide the necessary epitexts, in terms of shelving space, to allow the books to find the market. In theory, this should have meant the end of new adult fiction. But, as this section will show, it did not.

This was precisely because of the tumult Thompson notes in the previously quoted passage. In the early 2010s, publishing was changing significantly, and the affordances of digital publishing provided new opportunities for the authors and the texts to find their readerships. However, the form of new adult fiction that emerged was not the one that St Martin's had initially envisioned, which was a generic melting pot whose defining features were protagonist age and intended demographic (thus operating as a genre in the same way as children's, middle-grade and young adult fiction). Rather, the texts that emerged as major new adult blockbusters all had strikingly similar plot features, aligning this new form of fiction much more strongly with a genre defined by its narrative trajectory: romance. This clearly demonstrates the fluidity of genre, and the ways in which there can be substantial bleed between categories determined primarily by implied readership and those by plot trajectory. Even though paratextual elements such as a category's name remain consistent, what that name denotes can change enormously in only a few years.

2.1 Failure to Launch? New Adult after the St Martin's Contest

As discussed in the previous section, the concept of new adult as a literary category lost some momentum after the St Martin's competition. We can attribute this to a number of things, including, but not limited to, the press's lack of acquisitions from the contest, the fact that no subsequent contests were held and the institutional obstacle in the question of shelving in retail booksellers. Also contributing to this is that traditional publishing is a slow process. The books that St Martin's did acquire in its 'new adult endeavour' (Jae-Jones 2011), such as Nora Zelevansky's *Semi-Charmed Life* and Gemma Burgess' *Brooklyn Girls*, were not published until 2012 and 2013 respectively (conveniently, as the rest of this section will make clear, in the middle of the new adult boom, although neither seems to have made the impact of some of the other texts I will discuss).

This is not to say the label disappeared. Weiss and Jae-Jones still continued to use it in interviews and to express their hope that 'new adult' might become common parlance for both a literary category and a demographic through 2010 and 2011 (Brown 2011; Jae-Jones 2011). Literary agent Vickie Motter (2011) described new adult as a '(slowly) emerging genre', noting that she hadn't 'read many New Adult books yet (though really, there aren't many out there)', but she would accept queries for new adult manuscripts, something that suggests that the term was still in circulation in at least some circles. Motter was more hopeful than some, however. In the same year, ex-agent and freelance editor Mary Kole wrote the following:

> The whole 'New Adult' 'trend' that we all heard about on Twitter a year ago is the work of one imprint (St Martin's) at one publishing house (Macmillan). It has failed to take off.... There is a Middle Grade (sometimes called Independent Reader) shelf and a Young Adult shelf at most bookstores. There is no New Adult shelf, and they're not sharpening their saws to build one anytime soon. (2011)

Once again, we see the spectre of the shelf – here, quite clearly a physical shelf, one that would require wood and a sharp saw to construct – as the sticking point. Even if authors write the books, even if readers want the books, without the epitextual function performed by the shelf, how are the authors to find the readers? The answer became clear quite soon after Kole made these remarks. If institutions would not provide the shelves, then communities would. The second wave of new adult fiction arose in large part because readers took taxonomies into their own hands. Grassroots digital shelving succeeded where physical shelving had not.

In particular, this happened via the literary social networking site Goodreads, a space where readers can '[create] a bibliocentric as well as an egocentric network of public reading performance' (Nakamura 2013, 240). Goodreads is not the only such site; however, it is the most well known and widely used, and so it provides useful data as to how readers are categorising texts. As I will discuss further, it also played an important role in the re-emergence of new adult after the initial St Martin's contest. For these reasons, I use Goodreads data throughout this Element as a way of examining the way readers were using and understanding the term 'new adult'.

Sites like Goodreads have multiple functions – as Simone Murray notes, they allow readers to make recommendations, to rate books and to connect with people with similar taste – but, most importantly for my purposes here, they '[allow] avid readers to catalogue and annotate their book collections' (2015, 324). The 2000s are often positioned as notable because they saw the digitisation of the book, a technological revolution that led to some of the widespread anxiety in the publishing industry referred to by Thompson (2012, xi). However, we should not miss that this period also saw the digitisation of the book*shelf* (Nakamura 2013, 240). In Goodreads and other literary social network sites, taxonomical functions previously performed by institutional forces like bookstores and libraries were democratised.

Goodreads shelves function as 'a forum for information sharing, a collocation device, a locus of inclusion and exclusion, and a readers' advisory tool' (Desrochers et al. 2013, 2). When a reader appends a label to a book, it is added to one of its bookshelves, which are the key feature of an individual user's space on the website (Albrechtslund 2019, 7). These bookshelves are not demarcated solely by genre. Shelves like currently-reading, to-read, books-I-own and dnf (did not finish) are commonly utilised by Goodreads users. However, as of the time of writing, the Goodreads interface features a sidebar on the right-hand side of any given book's page which displays the different generic shelves onto which users have sorted it, under the heading 'genres'. When I discuss the top three ways a text was shelved in this Element, I am referring specifically to the shelf labels that appear in this genre sidebar, not to more expansive shelving practices.

In theory, the Goodreads bookshelf is the analogue to an individual reader's bookshelf: it 'simulate[s] the physical shelf of the book aficionado' (Barnett 2015, 14) and is a space where a reader can advertise a reading self. Generally, though, physical bookshelves are located in the private space of the home – as Lisa Nakamura notes, '[c]ruising a bookshelf at a party is a licensed form of surveillance' (2013, 240). By contrast, the logics of social networking sites are, of course, social, which means that a reader's individual shelving choices can have broader cataloguing implications.

This practice is not without issues: as Desrochers et al. note, 'problems with social tagging abound, with users tagging content in often idiosyncratic ways without giving much consideration to existing best practices, obtained from years of research in library and information science' (2016, 1028). The categories created are thus 'folksonomies' (Pennington & Spiteri 2018; Veros 2019), rather than formal taxonomies. However, much as the distinction between 'genre' and 'marketing category' is functionally irrelevant in the physical space of the bookstore, so too is the distinction between 'folksonomy' and 'taxonomy' in the digital space of Goodreads. While we should be wary of overstating the individual reader's power – Murray rightly notes that we should also consider factors like the political economy of the parent company and the role of the algorithm when considering Goodreads and similar sites (2019, 5) – there is little doubt that the folksonomical social tagging practices that occur in Goodreads can engender possibilities for readers to shape and direct the evolution of genres.

This is in clear evidence if we examine the re-emergence of new adult fiction post-2009. It is not possible to precisely identify exactly when readers began to shelve books as 'new adult' on Goodreads, but the term certainly seems to have remained in the collective memories of readerships in the wake of the St Martin's contest. Some of the books readers began to shelve as new adult included traditionally published texts that had been marketed as young adult, such as Gayle Forman's *Where She Went*, Kody Keplinger's *The Duff* and Richelle Mead's *Bloodlines* (as of May 2020, *Where She Went* had been shelved as new adult 318 times, *The Duff* 144 times, and *Bloodlines* 28 times). The new adult label slowly became more prevalent in 2011, especially for self-published contemporary romances. Texts like S. C. Stephens' *Thoughtless*; Jessica Park's *Flat-Out Love*; and, most importantly, Jamie McGuire's *Beautiful Disaster* – which was to become the first of numerous major self-published new adult breakout bestsellers – were all shelved numerous times as new adult (as of May 2020, *Thoughtless* had been shelved as new adult 1,103 times, *Flat-Out Love* 657 times and *Beautiful Disaster* 2,927 times). According to Goodreads founder Elizabeth Chandler,

2011 saw an explosion of popularity for the term 'new adult' on the site, with the number of readers recommending books bearing the new adult label exploding from 'a negligible amount to more than 14,000' (Kaufman 2012).

It is difficult – perhaps impossible – to determine the correlation between the exponential growth of books being shelved as new adult and books being written directly for the new adult market. Given that the term was popularised by St Martin's at the end of 2009, it is a relatively reasonable assumption that books written to fulfil that market might begin to be (especially self-) published in notable numbers from approximately 2011 onwards. However, we should note that as some of the case studies that follow will show, authors often applied the new adult label to their work *after* it began being shelved that way on Goodreads, suggesting that their books were not necessarily intentionally being written to satisfy the concept of new adult as put forward by St Martin's. As I will discuss further in this section, the vast majority of the books that were published as new adult during the boom period were contemporary romance. Romance has a particular reputation for industry savviness – see, for instance, its swift adoption and deft exploitation of the affordances of digital publishing in the 2000s (McAlister 2020) – and so it is perhaps not surprising that this was the genre that was best able to capitalise on the momentum of the term 'new adult'.

At any rate, what is very clear is that from 2011 onwards, the term 'new adult' began to be applied to books exponentially. If nothing else, this made it *seem* like there was an explosion of content in this subgene. According to the bibliographic website FictionDB, 46 new adult books were published in 2010, 218 in 2011, 604 in 2012, and more than 1,000 in 2013. This period, in which new adult books began to penetrate bestseller lists, is what I have termed the 'new adult boom' (McAlister 2018a).

2.2 The Second Coming of Chick Lit?

As discussed at length in the first section, St Martin's envisioned new adult as a generic melting pot, defined almost entirely by the target demographic. In particular, Jae-Jones was explicit that while chick lit might come under the purview of new adult, new adult should not *only* be chick lit, and the coining of the term 'new adult' was not an attempt to 'try and revive a dead genre with a sexy new name' (2009e). However, with few exceptions, the texts that emerged in the new adult boom – in particular, the ones that began to use the term 'new adult' in their paratexts – belonged, if not to chick lit, to a close relative: contemporary romance.

These forms are similar but not identical, so I would like to devote a little bit of space here to unpacking the difference between them. Romance fiction is a form defined largely by plot features. According to the Romance Writers of America, a romance novel must have two things: a 'central love story' and an 'emotionally satisfying and optimistic ending' (RWA n.d.). The latter is almost always HEA (happily ever after) or HFN (happy for now). Similarly, Pamela Regis contends that a romance novel is 'a work of prose fiction that tells the story of the courtship and betrothal of one or more heroines' (2003, 19), a definition she has since updated to be more inclusive, replacing 'heroines' with 'protagonists' (2011). Romance fiction is a broad generic umbrella and includes innumerable subgenres. One of the most notable of these is contemporary romance – that is, romance set in the present day as of the time of writing.

Chick lit has many overlaps with contemporary romance, in that books in this genre are resolutely contemporary: chick lit scholars Suzanne Ferriss and Mallory Young borrow a definition from journalist Heather Cabot and state that 'chick lit features single women in their twenties and thirties "navigating their generation's challenges of balancing demanding careers with personal relationships"' (2013, 3). That focus on personal relationships means that chick lit books often include romance: think here, for instance, of chick lit classic *Bridget Jones' Diary* (1996), which details Bridget's relationships with both Daniel Cleaver and Mark Darcy. Bridget and Mark end the novel together, meaning that the book fulfils the emotionally satisfying and optimistic ending requirement of the romance novel. However, the centrality of the love plot is where chick lit and contemporary romance tend to diverge. While I would not wholly agree with Ferriss and Young's reported claim that 'chick lit jettisons the heterosexual hero to offer a more realistic portrait of single life, dating, and the dissolution of romantic ideals' (2013, 3), given that said heterosexual hero is certainly a constant presence in chick lit, the romance between him and the heroine is not necessarily the primary driving feature of the plot. This is clear in *Bridget Jones' Diary*, as well as in another chick lit classic, Sophie Kinsella's *The Secret Dreamworld of a Shopaholic* (2000).[3] The romance between heroine Becky Bloomwood and hero Luke Brandon is a strong subplot but not *the* plot: that revolves more around Becky's addiction to shopping. Indeed, their romance progresses throughout the course of the series, and in later books, they are married with children. This locates the later books in what An Goris (2013) has called the 'post-HEA' space, meaning that the work of the romance narrative is done, but still, the plot continues, demonstrating that the love plot is not necessarily the driving force behind chick lit.

One key reason many wondered whether the 2009 St Martin's version of new adult would supplant chick lit was that the latter was, at the time, in decline. Heike Missler (2016, 41) contends that sales dropped across the publishing industry because of the 2009 recession, and so widespread claims that chick lit was dead were hyperbolic; however, there is no doubt that this genre was well and truly declining in popularity by the later 2000s. New adult was not intended by St Martin's to be a new moniker for chick lit; however, if we examine the books that began to be shelved as new adult and then hit bestseller lists, it seems quite clear that the new adult of the boom period was fulfilling some of the same needs. It was not directly analogous to chick lit – the books that emerged were predominantly contemporary romance and so had that stronger focus on a love plot that chick lit historically had not – but the overlap was pronounced enough for literary agent Kristin Nelson to call new adult 'perhaps the latest word for chick lit' (2013) and author Megan Westfield to describe it as 'simply chick lit that has expanded beyond its own negative stereotype of stilettos, martinis, and Manhattan' (2017).

2.3 The New Adult Boom: Key Moments, Key Authors

I have written about the new adult boom so far in quite general terms. This section is devoted to a more granular examination of the phenomenon, combining qualitative case studies of key authors and quantitative data

---

[3] Published as *Confessions of a Shopaholic* in some territories, and adapted into a film of the same name.

drawn from the *New York Times* bestseller list, so as to explore how the genre developed in this period.

I have used the *New York Times* list for two key reasons. Firstly, it is widely recognised as the most influential list in the publishing industry, making it a good measure to see how far a text or a genre has penetrated into mainstream literary culture (Bao & Chang 2014; Korda 2001; Sorensen 2007). Secondly, during the period under examination, it separated out its combined print and e-book bestseller lists from its e-book only lists. Self-publishing is a largely digital phenomenon, so tracking the transformation of self-published new adult e-books into traditional print-based books – importantly, in the case of new adult, books that might be sold in a physical bookstore – is an excellent way of demonstrating the impact that this category made during its boom.

To begin with key authors: as I discussed earlier, 2010 and 2011 saw use of the 'new adult' genre shelf label on Goodreads climb exponentially. Most notably, it began to be applied to self-published contemporary romance novels. While this happened across a broad spectrum of novels – and continued to happen well into 2012 and 2013, as the *New York Times* data will show –we can point to two key authors whose work really penetrated the mainstream and began the snowball that would become the new adult boom rolling: Jamie McGuire and Colleen Hoover.

2.3.1 Jamie McGuire

In late May 2011, Jamie McGuire self-published *Beautiful Disaster* as an e-book. This was not her first foray into self-publishing: at the end of 2010, she had self-published *Providence*, the first book in her paranormal romance series of the same name. *Beautiful Disaster* was, however, her first foray into contemporary romance.

Set on a college campus, *Beautiful Disaster* is a good girl/bad boy romance told in the first person between virginal first-year college student Abby Abernathy (the heroine and perspective character) and underground MMA fighter Travis Maddox, 'the ultimate college campus charmer' and 'Eastern University's Walking One Night Stand' (McGuire 2012a). Travis is drawn to Abby because she is one of the few women who does not want to date him. Despite Abby's distaste for his reputation, they begin to develop a friendship, one that positions her as different from the other women in his life: in his words, 'I don't want to sleep with you, Pidge [Pigeon, a nickname Travis gives Abby]. I like you too much' (McGuire 2012a, 43). Their relationship is heightened when they make a bet that results in Abby living with Travis in his apartment for a month. After sleeping together on the final night, they begin a tumultuous on-again off-again relationship, which culminates in them nearly dying in a fire. This near-death experience solidifies their commitment, and the novel ends with them having returned from Las Vegas as newlyweds, he tattooed with her nickname, Pigeon, and she with her married name, Mrs Maddox.

It seems as if McGuire initially intended to market *Beautiful Disaster* as contemporary romance. Certainly, it does not appear as if she had any intent of marketing it as new adult. Before its publication, she described it as a 'Women's Fiction novel' (McGuire 2011); even well after its publication, she described it as 'contemporary romance' in her website FAQ (McGuire 2012b). However, readers quickly began to shelve the book using the 'new adult' label on Goodreads. The first instance of this label being appended to the book that I could find was on 10 June 2011, only two weeks after its publication (Monika 2011). As of the time of writing in May 2020, it has been shelved as new adult 2,927 times (its second most common genre label; the first is romance, with 5,388 users shelving it as such).

Beautiful Disaster did well enough that McGuire was able to self-publish a trade paperback edition in October 2011 (something not very common in self-publishing in this period, due to distribution issues – while bricks-and-mortar bookstores can sometimes order self-published print books if readers request them, they will rarely carry them otherwise). From there, the buzz around the book continued to build. On 20 May 2012, the book appeared on the *New York Times* e-book fiction bestseller list at #22. It remained on the list for eight consecutive weeks, peaking at #9 on 8 July 2012. That week, it also appeared on the combined print and e-book fiction bestseller list at #13: a substantial achievement for a book whose only print edition was self-published.

Later that month, after a bidding war, McGuire was signed by Atria Books (an imprint of Simon & Schuster) for a two-book deal, which encompassed the republication of *Beautiful Disaster* in print and digital, and a retelling of the book from hero Travis' point of view called *Walking Disaster* (Deahl 2012a). The press releases that announced the signing claimed that 200,000 copies of *Beautiful Disaster* had already been sold (Deahl 2012a). No doubt anxious to capitalise on the momentum the book had, Atria's republication of *Beautiful Disaster* was speedy. The traditionally published version reappeared on the *New York Times* bestseller list in early September, spending two weeks on the combined print and e-book fiction list (charting at #13 on 2 September 2012[4] and #11 on 9 September 2012) and one week on the e-book fiction list (charting at #24 on 9 September 2012). When the follow-up *Walking Disaster* was published, it debuted at #1 on the *New York Times* combined print and e-book fiction bestseller list, the paperback trade fiction list and the e-book fiction list for 21 April 2013. It did not have as long a list life as its predecessor, but it spent two weeks total on all three lists. Later books in the series – the novella *A Beautiful Wedding* and *Beautiful Oblivion*, which focused on one of Travis' brothers – also made the combined print and e-book fiction and e-book fiction bestseller lists in 2014. By any measure, McGuire's books, which began as self-published e-books, enjoyed enormous success in the mainstream literary marketplace, including in print editions.

Publisher's Weekly suggested that Atria's acquisition of *Beautiful Disaster* and the at-that-point unwritten companion books might have been motivated by a desire to recreate the *Fifty Shades* phenomenon: they '[spared] no opportunity to compare the book to that other well known self-published phenomenon topping bestseller lists' (Deahl 2012a). There are indeed some similarities between the two. A case can also be made that the success of *Fifty Shades* – which began as fan fiction, was republished as original fiction through a boutique small press and was then acquired and republished by a major imprint (McAlister 2020) – paved the way for *Beautiful Disaster* and the new adult boom that was to follow. However, the two texts were positioned as forerunners of different distinct literary

---

[4] The publisher was given as McGuire in this first week; it is unclear whether this was an error by the *New York Times*.

categories. EL James and *Fifty Shades* kickstarted a wave of erotic romance penetrating bestseller lists. McGuire, however, was ultimately positioned as one of the first and foremost authors in the concurrent boom in new adult. As of the time of writing in May 2020, McGuire's official bio on her website states that she 'paved the way for the New Adult genre with the international bestseller *Beautiful Disaster*' (McGuire 2020).

2.3.2 Colleen Hoover

If McGuire is the first self-published author to make the *New York Times* bestseller lists with a new adult book, Hoover is arguably one of, if not the, most successful, with three self-published books charting, as well as numerous others once she had been signed by a major publisher.

Hoover self-published her debut novel *Slammed* in January 2012 and followed it swiftly with the sequel *Point of Retreat* in February 2012. Unlike *Beautiful Disaster*, which was always positioned for an adult romance market, *Slammed* in particular was positioned as young adult romance. It takes place during eighteen-year-old heroine Layken's final year in high school. After moving to a new town with her mother and younger brother following her father's death, Layken befriends her twenty-one-year-old neighbour Will. They form an immediate bond, only for this to be derailed when the school year starts and Layken discovers Will is her English teacher. They fight their attraction over the course of the book, while also bonding over slam poetry, about which Will teaches her. After he resigns his teaching job and takes another, and she responds to the urging of her terminally ill mother to use her heart instead of her head, Will and Layken end the book together. They face more obstacles to their relationship in the sequel *Point of Retreat*, which takes place a year later, but they also end that book as an established romantic couple.

Slammed was initially described as 'young adult' on Hoover's website (2012), and the age of the protagonist and the high school setting would seem to position it in that category (although Layken is nineteen and out of school by the time of *Point of Retreat*). However, as with *Beautiful Disaster*, readers quickly began applying the 'new adult' label to both books on Goodreads. The first instance of this label being appended to *Slammed* that I could find occurred on 15 March 2012, two months after its initial publication (Hannah 2012), and to *Point of Retreat* on 5 April 2012, also two months after its initial publication (Elle 2012).

As with *Beautiful Disaster*, *Slammed* and *Point of Retreat* began to garner significant readerships based on word of mouth. Goodreads seems to have facilitated this process: Elizabeth Chandler, the founder of Goodreads, claims that Hoover 'credits the book's [*Slammed*] success widely to Goodreads' (Narula 2014). Six months after its initial publication, *Slammed* debuted on the *New York Times* e-book fiction bestseller list, charting at #13 on 22 July 2012. A week later on 29 July 2012, it debuted at #15 on the combined print and e-book fiction list. In total, *Slammed* charted on the e-book list for six consecutive weeks, peaking at #8, and on the combined print and e-book list for five. *Point of Retreat* also charted on the e-book list, debuting at #19 on 29 July 2012 and remaining there for five weeks, peaking at #18. As with *Beautiful Disaster*, *Slammed* in particular made a demonstrable impact in the traditional literary marketplace, charting on the *New York Times* list for several weeks as a self-published book.

In almost an exact copy of what happened with McGuire in July 2012, Atria signed Hoover in August 2012 after a bidding war described as 'heated', in a deal that encompassed the republication of both *Slammed* and *Point of Retreat* in print and digital (Atria Books 2012). This was not, however, Hoover's last foray into self-publishing. In December 2012, she self-published *Hopeless*.

In this novel, the heroine, seventeen-year-old Sky, has moved to a new town with her guardian Karen and encounters the hero, Holder, who seems to recognise her even though they have, to her knowledge, never met before. They are enrolled in the same high school and, after gradually discussing elements of their respectful painful pasts, form a romantic relationship. However, Sky eventually discovers that this is not the first time she has met Holder: they knew each other as children, in a period that she can only barely remember, when her name was Hope, not Sky. They work together to uncover Sky's repressed memories of childhood sexual abuse, and the novel's climax comes when they confront her long-lost abusive father, who eventually dies by suicide. The novel ends with Sky's guardian Karen confessing that she kidnapped Sky to save her life and Sky thanking her, and with Sky and Holder together as an established couple.

Like *Slammed*, *Hopeless* was a contemporary romance that could easily be positioned as young adult, due to the age of the protagonist and the high school setting. However, also like *Slammed*, it began to be shelved as new adult quickly: the first instance I could find came from June 2012, six months *prior* to publication, presumably as a reaction to an advance review copy (AJ 2012). *Hopeless* debuted on the *New York Times* e-book fiction bestseller list at #19 on 6 January 2013 – two weeks after publication – and remained there for eleven consecutive weeks, peaking at #1 for three weeks from 20 January to 3 February 2013. It also appeared on the combined print and e-book fiction bestseller list, debuting on 13 January 2013 at #5 and remaining there for seven consecutive weeks, including three weeks (also 20 January to 3 February 2013) at #2: quite an achievement for a book that did not at that stage have a print edition. In late January 2013, Hoover signed a deal for *Hopeless* with Atria, giving it the rights to produce a print edition but retaining control of the digital edition herself (Associated Press 2013). This is quite an unusual publishing deal and speaks directly to the success that *Hopeless* was having in the wider literary marketplace without institutional backing. Given its success, it makes sense that Hoover sought to keep the digital rights, wherein she would retain a much greater portion of the profit.

Four more books from Hoover – *This Girl* (a follow up to *Slammed* and *Point of Retreat*), *Losing Hope* (a follow up to *Hopeless*), *Maybe Someday* and *Ugly Love* – would all go on to appear on the *New York Times* combined print and e-book fiction bestseller list in 2013–14. As of the time of writing in May 2020, her website describes her novels as '[falling] into the New Adult and Young Adult contemporary romance categories' (Hoover 2020). Notably, this includes three separate genre terms, which demonstrates, arguably, Hoover's agility at mobilising labels in service of promoting her work, depending on the fluctuations of the market.

2.3.3 The Boom

McGuire and Hoover were among the earliest authors who broke into the *New York Times* bestseller list with works that had been labelled 'new adult' by readers. Another author who charted with a self-published novel during the same period was Tammara Webber with *Easy*, a first-person contemporary romance novel in which heroine Jacqueline, isolated at her college after being dumped by her boyfriend, falls in love again after being sexually assaulted. *Easy* did not chart as highly as the works of McGuire and Hoover on the *New York Times* bestseller list – it did not make the combined print and e-book fiction bestseller list – but it appeared for three consecutive weeks on the e-book fiction list, peaking at #19 on 8 July 2012. Webber was also swiftly signed by a major publisher, with UK/Commonwealth and North American rights sold to various divisions of Penguin in September and October 2012, respectively. Notably, the term 'new adult' was used in material about the acquisition: for instance, *Publisher's Weekly* announcement about the acquisition of North American rights used the term and described it as 'publishing speak for books that usually feature characters slightly beyond their teenage years' (Deahl 2012b).

From here, a wave of similar books – self-published contemporary romance, usually first person, generally set on a college campus or featuring college-aged characters – swamped the *New York Times* bestseller list. They particularly dominated the e-book fiction list, but several also penetrated the combined print and e-book fiction list: especially notable because, as mentioned earlier, many of these books did not have print editions and formal distribution. Just as *Beautiful Disaster* and *Slammed* were beginning to fall down the lists, new books rose to take their places, such as *Down to You* by M. Leighton, *The Secret of Ella and Micha* and *The Coincidence of Callie and Kayden* by Jessica Sorensen, and *The Edge of Never* by J.A. Redmerski, all self-published, all frequently shelved as new adult on Goodreads. Table Group 5 shows all the books with new adult in their top three Goodreads genre shelf labels that appeared in the top fifteen on the *New York Times* combined print and e-book bestseller list between 2012 and 2014. This demonstrates the extent to which new adult became a genuine publishing phenomenon in this period: particularly because, as I mentioned, many of these books did not yet have print editions, at least in their self-published incarnations.

This table group, obviously, is quite lengthy. If I were to include a similar table group that encompassed all the books shelved as new adult that appeared on the *New York Times* bestseller list for e-book fiction for the same period, it would almost triple in size. I have not used the term 'boom' to describe this

Table 5 New adult bestsellers according to the *New York Times* combined print and e-book fiction list (encompassing top fifteen books per week), 2012–14.

Table 5(a) 2012

Title	Author	Publisher	List Debut	Peaked at	Total Weeks on List	Top Three Goodreads Gnre Shelf Labels
Beautiful Disaster	McGuire, Jamie	Self (later Atria)	8 July 2012	#11	3	1. Romance 2. New adult 3. Contemporary
Slammed	Hoover, Colleen	Self (later Atria)	29 July 2012	#10	5	1. Romance 2. New adult 3. Young adult
Down to You	Leighton, M.	Self (later Berkley)	21 October 2012	#12	3	1. Romance 2. New adult 3. Contemporary
The Secret of Ella and Micha	Sorensen, Jessica	Self (later Forever)	11 November 2012	#6	4	1. New adult 2. Romance 3. Contemporary
The Edge of Never	Redmerski, J.A.	Self (later Grand Central)	16 December 2012	#9	4	1. Romance 2. New adult 3. Contemporary

Table 5(b) 2013 – January to June

Title	Author	Publisher	List Debut	Peaked at	Total Weeks on List	Top Three Goodreads Gnre Shelf Labels
The Coincidence of Callie and Kayden	Sorensen, Jessica	Self (later Forever)	6 January 2013	#3	6	1. Romance 2. New adult 3. Contemporary
Hopeless	Hoover, Colleen	Self (later Atria)	13 January 2013	#2	7	1. Romance 2. New adult 3. Young adult
Someone to Love	Moore, Addison	Self (later Skyscape)	20 January 2013	#6	4	1. Romance 2. New adult 3. Academic > college
Collide	McHugh, Gail	Self (later Atria)	17 February 2013	#6	1	1. Romance 2. New adult 3. Romance > contemporary romance

Table 5(b) Cont.

Title	Author	Publisher	List Debut	Peaked at	Total Weeks on List	Top Three Goodreads Gnre Shelf Labels
Lost to You	Jackson, A.L.	Sapphire Star Publishing (micro-press)	24 February 2013	#11	1	1. Romance 2. New adult 3. Romance > contemporary romance
If You Stay	Cole, Courtney	Self (later Forever)	3 March 2013	#9	2	1. New adult 2. Romance 3. Contemporary
Hard to Resist	Williams, Shanora	Self	10 March 2013	#15	1	1. New adult 2. Romance > contemporary romance 3. Contemporary
Fallen Too Far	Glines, Abbi	Self (later Atria)	17 March 2013	#12	3	1. Romance 2. New adult 3. Contemporary
Reckless	Stephens, S.C.	Simon & Schuster	24 March 2013	#1	1	1. Romance 2. New adult 3. Contemporary

Title	Author	Publisher	Date			Genre
Wait for You	Lynn, J.	Self (later Morrow/ HarperCollins)	24 March 2013	#2	4	1. New adult 2. Romance 3. Contemporary
Never Too Far	Glines, Abbi	Self (later Atria)	31 March 2013	#15	1	1. Romance 2. New adult 3. Contemporary
Falling into You	Wilder, Jasinda	Self	7 April 2013	#6	4	1. Romance 2. New adult 3. Contemporary
Walking Disaster	McGuire, Jamie	Atria	21 April 2013	#1	2	1. Romance 2. New adult 3. Contemporary
The Bet	Van Dyken, Rachel	Self (later Forever)	28 April 2013	#1	6	1. Romance 2. New adult 3. Contemporary
Damaged	Ward, H.M.	Laree Bailey (self-publishing entity)	28 April 2013	#2	4	1. Romance 2. New adult 3. Contemporary
Real	Evans, Katy	Self (later Gallery)	5 May 2013	#5	3	1. Romance 2. New adult 3. Contemporary

Table 5(b) Cont.

Title	Author	Publisher	List Debut	Peaked at	Total Weeks on List	Top Three Goodreads Gnre Shelf Labels
Twisted Perfection	Glines, Abbi	Self (later Atria)	12 May 2013	#6	2	1. New adult 2. Romance 3. Contemporary
This Girl	Hoover, Colleen	Atria	19 May 2013	#10	1	1. Romance 2. New adult 3. Contemporary
Down London Road	Young, Samantha	NAL	26 May 2013	#14	1	1. Romance 2. New adult 3. Romance > contemporary romance
The Forever of Ella and Micha	Sorensen, Jessica	Forever	16 June 2013	#5	1	1. New adult 2. Romance 3. Contemporary
A Different Blue	Harmon, Amy	Self	16 June 2013	#13	1	1. Romance 2. New adult 3. Contemporary

Table 5(c) 2013 – July to December

Title	Author	Publisher	List Debut	Peaked at	Total Weeks on List	Top Three Goodreads Gnre Shelf Labels
Forever Too Far	Glines, Abbi	Self (later Atria)	7 July 2013	#4	2	1. New adult 2. Romance 3. Contemporary
Damaged 2	Ward, H.M.	Laree Bailey (self-publishing entity)	14 July 2013	#2	1	1. Romance 2. New adult 3. Contemporary
Losing Hope	Hoover, Colleen	Atria	28 July 2013	#7	1	1. Romance 2. New adult 3. Young adult
Pulse	McHugh, Gail	Self (later Atria)	28 July 2013	#9	3	1. Romance 2. New adult 3. Romance > contemporary romance
The Redemption of Callie and Kayden	Sorensen, Jessica	Forever	18 August 2013	#2	1	1. New adult 2. Romance 3. Contemporary

Table 5(c) Cont.

Title	Author	Publisher	List Debut	Peaked at	Total Weeks on List	Top Three Goodreads Gnre Shelf Labels
Stripped	Ward, H.M.	Laree Bailey (self-publishing entity)	22 September 2013	#10	1	1. Romance 2. New adult 3. Contemporary
Out of Line	McLaughlin, Jen	Self	6 October 2013	#10	1	1. New adult 2. Romance 3. Contemporary
Simple Perfection	Glines, Abbi	Atria	13 October 2013	#8	1	1. New adult 2. Romance 3. Contemporary
The Temptation of Lila and Ethan	Sorensen, Jessica	Forever	10 November 2013	#4	1	1. New adult 2. Romance 3. Contemporary
The Edge of Always	Redmerski, J.A.	Forever	24 November 2013	#5	1	1. New adult 2. Romance 3. Contemporary
Remy	Evans, Katy	Forever	15 December 2013	#8	1	1. Romance 2. New adult 3. Warfare > fighters

Title	Author	Publisher	Date			Genres
Forever Us	Lynn, Sandi	Self	15 December 2013	#10	1	1. Romance 2. Romance > contemporary romance 3. New adult
The Ever After of Ella and Micha	Sorensen, Jessica	Forever	22 December 2013	#15	1	1. New adult 2. Romance 3. Romance > contemporary romance
A Beautiful Wedding	McGuire, Jamie	Atria	29 December 2013	#11	1	1. Romance 2. New adult 3. Contemporary

Table 5(d) 2014 – January to June

Title	Author	Publisher	List Debut	Peaked at	Total Weeks on List	Top Three Goodreads Gnre Shelf Labels
Rome	Crownover, Jay	Morrow / Harper Collins	26 January 2014	#12	1	1. Romance 2. New adult 3. Contemporary
Be With Me	Lynn, J.	Morrow / Harper Collins	23 February 2014	#5	1	1. New adult 2. Romance 3. Contemporary
Take a Chance	Glines, Abbi	Atria	16 March 2014	#7	1	1. New adult 2. Romance 3. Contemporary
Maybe Someday	Hoover, Colleen	Atria	6 April 2014	#4	1	1. Romance 2. New adult 3. Contemporary
Play	Scott, Kylie	St Martin's Griffin	13 April 2014	#11	1	1. Romance 2. New adult 3. Romance > contemporary romance

Title	Author	Publisher	Date	#		Categories
Nash	Crownover, Jay	Morrow/HarperCollins	18 May 2014	#9	1	1. Romance 2. New adult 3. Contemporary
Archer's Voice	Sheridan, Mia	Self (later Forever)	25 May 2014	#10	1	1. Romance 2. New adult 3. Contemporary
Rush Too Far	Glines, Abbi	Atria	25 May 2014	#12	1	1. New adult 2. Romance 3. Contemporary

Table 5(e) 2014 – July to December

Title	Author	Publisher	List Debut	Peaked at	Total Weeks on List	Top Three Goodreads Gnre Shelf Labels
Beautiful Oblivion	McGuire, Jamie	Atria	20 July 2014	#4	1	1. Romance 2. New adult 3. Contemporary
Where I Belong	Daniels, J.	Self	27 July 2014	#13	1	1. Romance 2. New adult 3. Contemporary
Addicted	Wolff, Tracy	Loveswept	3 August 2014	#13	1	1. Romance 2. Romance > contempor-ary romance 3. New adult
Lead	Scott, Kylie	St Martin's Griffin	17 August 2014	#6	1	1. Romance 2. New adult 3. Contemporary

Title	Author	Publisher	Date			Categories
Ugly Love	Hoover, Colleen	Atria	24 August 2014	#6	1	1. Romance 2. New adult 3. Contemporary
One More Chance	Glines, Abbi	Atria	21 September 2014	#11	1	1. New adult 2. Romance 3. Contemporary
Stepbrother Dearest	Ward, Penelope	Self	19 October 2014	#6	4	1. Romance 2. New adult 3. Contemporary
Rowdy	Crownover, Jay	Morrow/HarperCollins	9 November 2014	#8	1	1. Romance 2. New adult 3. Contemporary
You Were Mine	Glines, Abbi	Atria	21 December 2014	#12	1	1. Romance 2. New adult 3. Contemporary

period lightly: during this time, new adult became a genuine phenomenon. It was not simply a few breakout texts. It was a whole breakout genre.

If we examine Table Group 5 closely, we can see several patterns begin to emerge. The first is in the extreme commonality of genre shelf labels applied to these books. Fifty-seven books are included in this table; for almost all of them, the top three Goodreads genre shelf labels are 'romance', 'new adult', and 'contemporary'. During this period, when a book was shelved as new adult by readers, it was very clear what kind of book it was: a contemporary romance novel.[5] I can confirm this from my own reading across the new adult books of the boom. The plot trajectory of the romance novel, with its central love story and mandatory happy ending, is ubiquitous.

In other words, the generic melting pot envisioned by St Martin's was no more. New adult was entirely subsumed by the romance genre, moving it almost completely from being a genre defined by intended reader to one defined by plot trajectory. A new adult novel during this period was almost always a contemporary romance novel, usually featuring protagonists of college age, generally told in the first person of one or both protagonists. This shift in genre logics began in large part due to the folksonomical digital shelving practices of Goodreads users, which started this snowball of generic development rolling and then continued as authors were given more and more examples of what new adult fiction was. New adult fiction is thus an excellent example of how social formations can profoundly shape the processes of genre.

We should not, however, discount the influence of industry. While readers might have started the snowball rolling, we can see industrial forces swiftly coming on board and crystallising this new form of new adult. Table Group 5 tells the same story multiple times: self-published authors publishing extremely popular novels that are shelved as new adult by readers and then acquired and republished by traditional publishers, ensuring that the reach of the books grows and the snowball gains momentum. Particular imprints and publishers were particularly powerful institutional forces here:

---

[5] Notably, the only books shelved as young adult are Colleen Hoover's, demonstrating that the initial association between young adult and new adult had become tenuous at best during this period.

Atria (an imprint of Simon & Schuster) acquired not just McGuire and Hoover but also Abbi Glines, who wrote nine out of the fifty-seven books in Table Group 5. Forever (an imprint of Grand Central, part of Hachette) invested in new adult self-publishing successes Jessica Sorensen, J.A. Redmerski, Katy Evans, Courtney Cole and Rachel van Dyken; while William Morrow (part of HarperCollins) did the same for J. Lynn and Jay Crownover. We can argue that when the term 'new adult' was initially deployed by industry – that is, in the St Martin's competition – it failed, and it only succeeded when it was deployed by readerships, leading to this boom period.

But succeed it did, allowing books bearing the new adult label to find a readership hungry for them. Thus, industry was clearly glad to adopt the term as an institutional classification. In 2013, 'new adult' became an official Book Industry Standards and Communications (BISAC) category designation, giving it formal recognition (Naughton 2014, 20). BISAC codes are industrial taxonomical standards and 'can determine where the work is shelved in a brick-and-mortar store or the genre(s) under which it can be searched for in an internal database' (BISG n.d.). Shelving, we should remember, was an incredibly fraught question for the version of new adult conceived of by St Martin's, but the BISAC code for new adult provides a clear solution. The code is FIC027240: FICTION / Romance / New Adult. New adult fiction has become, for all formal taxonomical intents and purposes, a form of romance fiction.

The final pattern we can see in Table Group 5 is the gradual decline in popularity of new adult fiction. The peak was in 2013, especially in the first six months, when multiple books would regularly appear on the *New York Times* bestseller list. There were even some weeks when the genre would dominate the list: for instance, five of the fifteen books on the combined print and e-book fiction list for the week of 19 May 2013 were new adult, with an additional two appearing on the e-book fiction list. However, booms never last forever. During 2014, the momentum of this particular generic snowball began to taper off. With only a few exceptions, the authors who were charting on the lists had charted before: hardly any of the spectacular self-published breakouts were evident in late 2012–13. If we look past the list and into 2015, this momentum begins to fall even further. In the second half of 2015, only two books with new adult in their top three Goodreads genre shelf labels charted on the combined print and e-book bestseller list. One of these, *November 9*, was by one of new adult's initial breakout stars, Colleen Hoover, who had obviously by this time cultivated a substantial readership. However, unlike some of her works from the new adult boom, which charted near the top of the list for multiple weeks, *November 9* only charted on the combined list for one week, appearing at #10.

The new adult boom was undoubtedly formative for the genre. It is an extremely clear illustration of how the processes of genre are in constant flux, and how paratextual factors well outside the texts themselves can shape the way a genre is understood and the way it will develop. Claire Squires writes that '[w]hat ends up on which particular shelf, for how long and to what effect, are the questions that an examination of genre in the marketplace causes to be asked' (2007, 74). The examination of new adult that I have offered in this section functions as a case study to explore some of these questions and illuminates clearly the power that grassroots folksonomical practices, such as Goodreads shelving, have in shaping the way genres develop in the overall literary marketplace and are taken up by institutional forces.

But what happens when the interest of readers begins to wane? Where does genre go next? This will be the focus of my final section, as I look at the way new adult evolved from the boom period to the present.

3 2020 – New Adult, a Decade On

In his book *The Hidden Adult*, Perry Nodelman writes that he 'happily accept[s] the pragmatic definition that children's literature is the literature published as such' (2008, 147). He uses this definition as a way of accounting for the vast span of literature published for children, which encompasses many kinds of books, belonging to many plot-based genres, published in a plethora of ways and of vastly differing levels of quality and acclaim: '[a]ny acceptable view of the characteristic tendencies of children's literature as a genre will have to account in some way for all that vast range of apparently divergent texts,' he states (2008, 147).

If we were approaching new adult fiction from the perspective of a traveller from a parallel universe, one where the version of new adult as put forward by St Martin's had achieved broad recognition and not run into the institutional roadblock of the physical shelf, we might neatly substitute 'new adult' for 'children's literature' in these quotes from Nodelman. Apart from protagonist age, this version of new adult did not have any defining generic features beyond its target audience. As discussed in Section 1, it encompassed everything from literary fiction to fantasy to creative nonfiction to chick lit. In the parallel universe where this form of the genre had burst into being, it is extremely reasonable to assume that the publication of a book as new adult would determine whether or not it belonged to the category: that is, its paratextual features, rather than its textual features, would play the largest part in determining its genre.[6]

As Section 2 demonstrated, in our universe, this is not the version of new adult that emerged. Rather, driven by Goodreads shelving and self-publishing, new adult as of the boom period referred to texts that had distinct textual features, including specific plot trajectories: they were contemporary romance novels, usually with protagonists in college or of college age, and generally written in the first person from the perspective of one or both protagonists. The digital shelving practices of Goodreads may have begun as

---

[6] This paratextual paradox is not without precedent: see, for instance, Markus Zusak's *The Book Thief*, published as adult fiction in Australia and young adult in North America.

folksonomy, but as the books in this 'new' new adult began to hit major institutional bestseller lists, this form of the genre began to crystallise, and consistent textual practices began to emerge. That 'vast range of apparently divergent texts' that Nodelman notes in children's literature (2008, 147) and that St Martin's hoped to provoke in the new adult space did not eventuate: rather, we can talk about new adult shifting from being a genre based primarily on intended audience to one based on plot elements.

However, the fact that this boom period version of new adult had distinct textual features does not negate the important role that paratext plays in creating, shaping and determining genre. Claire Squires contends that 'the study of literature benefits greatly from investigations into the conditions of its production and reception' (2007, 7), a statement that has guided my examination of new adult. In particular, if we are to study genre, we must study paratext as well as text, because it is in these spaces that matters of production and reception are most visible: in peritexts (features that are included in the object of the book or e-book, such as covers and blurbs) and epitexts (features outside the object of the book or e-book, such as marketing materials and shelving, both institutional and folksonomical). Importantly, these paratexts are often created by forces outside the texts themselves (and often outside the authors of those texts as well). John Frow contends that '[g]enre is neither a property of (and located "in") texts, nor a projection of (and located "in") readers; it exists as part of the relationship between texts and readers, and it has a systemic existence. It is a shared convention with a social force' (2014, 160). I would, as Kim Wilkins (2005) has, add institutions to this list: as my discussion of the development of new adult fiction has shown, they play a key role in the formation and transformation of genres. But like texts and readers, institutions do not stand alone. It is in the *interactions* of industry, social formations, and texts that genres are shaped, reshaped, emerge and decline.

This section focuses on the books being published and classified as new adult as of the time of writing in 2020 to determine the state of the category in the present day. In order to do this, I have paired my own distant reading across the genre with a quantitative approach, examining data taken from Amazon bestseller lists and Goodreads to understand the state of new adult fiction as it currently stands. I am using Amazon bestseller lists here, rather than the *New York Times* bestseller lists I used in the previous section, because new adult has largely fallen out of the latter. It exists primarily in the domain of digital self-publishing, which the Amazon lists are much better placed to interrogate.

Nodelman writes that '[g]enres operate like schemata in two ways. First, readers develop their ideas about genres from previous experience of texts they see as fitting into them. Second, they use those ideas to understand the new texts they encounter' (2008, 109). By examining the Amazon and Goodreads data I have aggregated for the purposes of this section, we can gain a clearer picture of how readers are interacting with texts than we would by simply interrogating the texts themselves. We can see which texts being classified as new adult readers are buying; and the folksonomical shelving practices of Goodreads allow us to see what kind of texts readers are interpreting and classifying as new adult – two mutually reinforcing practices. From there, we can explore the relations of these texts to ideas about the genre from earlier periods – such as the two periods investigated in Sections 1 and 2 – so as to understand the intertextual relationships that have emerged between them and how the genre has developed. New adult is an especially interesting case study for this kind of work because it is a genre category that has undergone something of an identity crisis, as a result of (and, in some other ways, in spite of) the massive developments it has undergone in quite a condensed time frame. The new adult as envisioned by St Martin's and the new adult of the boom period are quite different, and we can see ideas arising from both versions clearly in the set of texts that currently carry the genre label.

3.1 Identity Crisis: New Adult as Fuzzy Set

As discussed at the end of the previous section, while new adult was enormously popular and regularly penetrated (and occasionally dominated) mainstream bestseller lists during its boom period, that popularity eventually began to wane. The numbers of new adult books being published did not necessarily decline dramatically: according to FictionDB, more than 1,000 new adult titles were published each year in 2013–18 (although interestingly, it only records 433 new adult titles published in 2019, and

282 as of the time of writing in 2020, which suggests that this decline might only have been postponed). However, despite the quantity of books, their visibility changed. Where new adult books made institutional bestseller lists like the *New York Times* list, they were typically by authors whose careers had been established during the boom period. New authors entering the new adult market did not enjoy such a precipitous rise to fame as some of their predecessors had only a few years prior.

The visibility of new adult during the boom period led to the crystallisation of the category's generic boundaries. All the books shelved by readers as new adult that made the bestseller lists were contemporary romances, focused on college-aged protagonists, usually in first person. As a result, new waves of books in the same mode were perpetuated and shelved by readers as new adult, thus reinforcing these generic boundaries. In addition, the explosion of popularity of new adult led to the authors who broke out during the boom swiftly serialising their books, often in quite complex ways. I have discussed elsewhere the serialisation practices that emerged during the boom – authors continuing series with the same characters, setting books in the same world but with different characters, or retelling successful books from different points of view (something Jamie McGuire and Colleen Hoover both notably did with success) – but what is most notable about this practice here is the way it further reinforced that new adult referred to a certain kind of text (McAlister 2018b).

We can see the influence of the boom clearly in Goodreads. In the platform's list of the top fifty books most shelved as new adult, the majority are from the boom period, as can be seen in Table 6.

It is reasonable, given this information, to assume that the new adult of the boom period played an enormous role in determining the future trajectory of the genre. The Goodreads most-shelved list may not exactly indicate a new adult canon, but it certainly points to the foundational texts of the genre, the ones that readers have most frequently understood as belonging to the genre. Given that the new adult of the boom period was a genre label for a fairly specific form of contemporary romance, it is likewise reasonable to assume that this trend would continue into the future.

This is true: as this section will show, new adult and first-person contemporary romance have continued to be relatively analogous.

Table 6 Publication dates for the top fifty books most commonly shelved as new adult in Goodreads, as of 2 June 2020

Year	Number of books from the top 50 list
2009	1
2010	0
2011	1
2012	12
2013	14
2014	7
2015	5
2016	6
2017	1
2018	1
2019	1

Note: There are only forty-nine books on this list, as Colleen Hoover's *Hopeless* appeared twice (two different editions).

However, when new adult slipped out of mainstream view, the generic boundaries established during the boom became a little less firm. While they were not destroyed, they certainly seem to have begun to erode. Brian Attebery famously discusses fantasy fiction and its various sub-genres as 'fuzzy sets', by which he meant that 'they are defined not by boundaries but by a center . . . a book on the fringes may be considered as belonging or not, depending on one's interests.. . . Furthermore, there may be no single quality that links an entire set' (1992, 12–13). If we apply this line of thought to new adult: the fiction of the boom period ultimately became not the arbiter of the category's *boundaries* but of its *centre*. This form of new adult – contemporary romance, college-aged protagonists, first person – became the most easily identifiable and categorised; however, as the genre slipped from view, the boundaries became increasingly fuzzy.

This fuzziness can be frustrating from a scholarly perspective, particularly if we wish to take a structuralist approach to the study of genre. However, as Marie-Laure Ryan asserts:

> As to the alleged fuzziness of the individual generic categories, it only constitutes a drawback if these notions are used as analytical tools. But if genres are an object rather than an instrument of investigation, if they are more or less entities themselves needing to be explained, then their fuzziness will no longer constitute a theoretical shortcoming, but a fact to account for. (1981, 110)

The growing fuzziness of new adult fiction is indeed, as Ryan states, something we have to account for. The genre's decline in visibility is certainly one reason for the boundaries beginning to blur. So is the return of the genre largely to the domain of self-publishing, which removes some institutional barriers to experimentation. However, one factor we should not negate the impact of is the residual memory of the 'original' version of new adult, the generic melting pot as envisioned by St Martin's. While that genre never exactly came to fruition, the re-emergence of the genre label during the boom period points to the extent to which it remained in literary consciousness, so it is thus not entirely surprising that elements of the original definition might also have continued to percolate and circulate.

3.2 New Adult Today: The Data

The publishing industry – especially when it comes to popular fiction, and even more so when it comes to self-publishing – moves incredibly quickly. The same is true of bestseller data in these spaces. While the *New York Times* bestseller list, which I used extensively in Section 2, is a weekly list, others are updated far more frequently, exponentially increasing the problem of 'immediate obsolescence' noted by John Thompson as troubling for scholars of publishing (2012, xi). The Amazon bestseller lists I am using in this section are updated every hour, so to keep track of them with any kind of completeness would be extremely difficult. I have chosen to take a snapshot approach: the data I captured is from 10 a.m. Australian Eastern Standard Time (AEST) on 2 June 2020. It is obviously not exhaustive or entirely representative; however, it still offers an interesting window into the state of new adult fiction at a given point in time.

The location of the bestseller lists in Amazon's own categorisation system is itself interesting when we consider the role that paratexts play in shaping how genres are understood. I am using the Best Sellers in New Adult and College Romance list, which is located under the Romance umbrella in Amazon's Kindle store. There is no alternative list for new adult located under any other generic umbrellas: new adult is clearly positioned here as a kind of romance. If we return to Attebery's (1992) notion of the fuzzy set, the romantic centre of this genre is extremely evident. Reading a little closer, we can also see the contemporary form of that romance inherent in the name of the list: 'college romance' quite definitely positions the texts in the present day.

Amazon offers two distinct bestseller lists, the top 100 paid books and the top 100 free books. These lists do not overlap substantially; so for the purposes of this section, I captured the first fifty books of each. The substantive reasons for this lack of overlap are out of the scope for any deep exploration in this section, but in brief: all fifty books on the paid list belong to Amazon's Kindle Unlimited program, a subscription-based library of books wherein authors give Amazon exclusivity. According to Mark Davis, this program 'functions as a "walled garden" for self-published authors who are tied to it by exclusivity agreements and for readers who gain access to books very cheaply' (2020, 97). Thus, it is extremely rare to find a book from a traditional publisher enrolled in the program. The free books list contains only ten books enrolled in the Kindle Unlimited program and features books published in a wider variety of modes, including traditional and non-Amazon exclusive self-published books that happened to have been made free by either publisher or author on the day I collected my data. The number of new adult books circulating in the Kindle Unlimited program suggests that this is a key site for the formation and reformation of the genre; however, relying solely on the paid bestseller list would suggest it is the only site, which is not the case.

I have cross-referenced these lists with Goodreads to best understand how readers are interpreting and categorising these books. I captured the top three genre shelf labels associated with each book (noting that some books have not been shelved by readers enough times to have had three labels appended, so the total label number is lower than 150). Tables 7 and 8 show how many times each genre shelf label has been used by readers in the corpus.

There are distinct similarities between the two lists. It is clear that romance continues to be the dominant overarching umbrella under which new adult fiction sits, meaning that for the most part, it is subject to the plot-based dictates of that genre (i.e. a central love story and a happy ending). Indeed, romance might be even more dominant than these tables suggest. Forty-three of the fifty books are shelved as romance on the paid list. Of the seven that are not, four have no genre shelf labels at all, which means they have not been shelved frequently enough in Goodreads for these to show up; however, even the quickest glance at the cover copy shows that they fit under the romance umbrella. Two more carry the label 'romance > contemporary romance', and the final one carries only one label – 'academic > college' – but again, even the most cursory reading reveals that it is a romance novel. On the free list, forty-nine out of the fifty books carry the romance genre shelf label. There is only one that does not, S.M. Reine's *The Tarot Witches I–IV*, which carries three fantasy labels. Its fourth Goodreads genre shelf label, however, is 'romance > paranormal romance': it too fits under the umbrella.

If we return to Attebery's (1992) notion of the fuzzy set, where a genre is defined by its centre rather than its boundaries, we can certainly see the centre writ clear in this data. New adult is still clearly dominated by romance fiction. This may be influenced by the nature of this particular bestseller list, which, as noted earlier, is specifically for 'new adult and college romance', but that in itself further reinforces the centre. In addition, contemporary romance continues to dominate: 'contemporary' and 'romance > contemporary romance' are the second- and third-largest genre shelf labels by a reasonable margin on both lists. There is obviously a little blurring of the boundaries occurring, with fantasy, paranormal and

Table 7 Goodreads genre shelf labels for top fifty books on Amazon Paid Bestseller List for New Adult and College Romance, 10 a.m. AEST 2 June 2020

Goodreads Genre Shelf Label	Number of Times Applied to Corpus
Academic > college	5
Adult	1
Adult fiction	1
Adult fiction > erotica	2
Contemporary	18
Contemporary romance > sports romance	2
Dark	4
Fairies > Fae	1
Fantasy	1
Fantasy > paranormal	1
Fiction	2
New adult	11
Paranormal > shapeshifters	1
Polyamorous > reverse harem	1
Romance	43
Romance > contemporary romance	16
Sports > sports	4
Suspense	1
Westerns	1
Young adult	1
Young adult > high school	3

some forms of erotic romance making some incursions into the generic space, but the centre remains clear and strong.

In some senses, this is quite an unremarkable finding. A genre had its breakout moment, and a few years down the track, it is carrying along in

Table 8 Goodreads genre shelf labels for top fifty books on Amazon Free Bestseller List for New Adult and College Romance, 10am AEST 2 June 2020

Goodreads Genre Shelf Label	Number of Times Applied to Corpus
Adult fiction > erotica	4
Business > Amazon	2
Contemporary	28
Dark	4
Fantasy	1
Fantasy > magic	1
Fantasy > paranormal	2
Fiction	2
Humor	1
Music	1
New adult	5
Paranormal > Omegaverse	1
Polyamorous > reverse harem	1
Romance	49
Romance > contemporary romance	27
Shapeshifters > werewolves	1
Sports > sports	3
Suspense	1
War > military fiction	1
Westerns	1
Women's fiction > chick lit	2

much the same way. But there is quite an unusual finding buried in this data that sets this 2020 form of new adult apart from the new adult of the boom: the gradual disappearance of the label 'new adult' itself.

Table Group 5 captured all the books on the *New York Times* Combined Print and E-book Fiction Bestseller List from 2012–14 for which 'new adult' featured in the top three genre shelf labels on Goodreads and noted that if I were to compile a similar list capturing only the E-book Fiction Bestseller list, it would be approximately three times longer. The new adult genre label was in high circulation on Goodreads and, as I showed in that section, was in constant companionship with labels such as 'romance', 'contemporary', and 'romance > contemporary romance'. However, for the books I have captured in my data in this section, which all appeared on a dedicated new adult romance bestseller list, 'new adult' appears relatively infrequently as a major genre shelf label. On the paid list, only eleven of the fifty books feature new adult in their top three genre shelf labels. On the free list, this number is even smaller: only five books feature it in their top three genre shelf labels. While they belong to the genre enough to be categorised that way for the institutional purposes of the Amazon bestseller lists – another indication of the strength of the generic centre established during the boom – the term 'new adult' seems to be falling into a level of disuse in reader spaces.

One way of reading this is that the genre label is simply disappearing. However, as its survival between the St Martin's competition and the boom period shows, it has historically been a term with some staying power. Moreover, the success of the boom led to its institutionalisation: as discussed in Section 2, 'new adult' is now a BISAC code, and, as the name of the Amazon list shows, it has become an accepted industry term. Use of the label might be declining, but to say that it is on the road to outright disappearance is, I think, somewhat hyperbolic.

An alternative reading is that the decline in application of this label to the Amazon bestsellers I have identified is another step in new adult's ongoing identity crisis. As shown earlier, the Amazon texts largely embody the centre of the generic fuzzy set, in that they are mostly contemporary romance novels. To gain an alternate perspective, I examined another list: the Goodreads 'most read this week in new adult' list, as of 2 June 2020, which contains the top 100 books shelved as new adult that the most users of the site had marked that they were reading or had read that week.

As with the Amazon bestseller lists, I captured the top three genre shelf labels for each of these books (noting that not every book has three labels, so the total number of labels is not 300). Table 9 shows how many times each label has been used by readers in this corpus.

The centre of the fuzzy set is still clear in this table: 84 of the 100 books on the list are shelved as romance. The genre shelf labels 'contemporary' and 'romance > contemporary romance' are also relatively popular. But this list also reveals some things different from the Amazon lists, which might indicate how new adult will come to be understood as a generic label in the future.

Perhaps the most notable finding is the significant proportion of books on the list that are not contemporary romance novels. In particular, fantasy novels seem to be making significant incursions into the new adult space, with 28 of the 100 books bearing the label. Several fantasy subgeneric classifications also appear on the list. Most are additional labels on books that already carry the fantasy genre shelf label, but we can add another book to the list of 28. This means that nearly a third of the books on the list are fantastical and thus do not adhere to the conventions of the new adult fiction that lie at the centre of the fuzzy set. Fantasy represents the biggest generic incursion, but it is worth noting that some other genres also appear on the edges, such as science fiction, mystery and thriller.

Another notable finding is the number of books on the list that carry the 'young adult' label. In the lengthy Table Group 5, which detailed the top three Goodreads genre shelf labels for all the new adult *New York Times* combined print and e-book fiction bestsellers from 2012–14, this label was quite rare: there were 57 books on the list, but 'young adult' only appeared in the top three labels for 3 of these books, all of which were by Colleen Hoover (who, as discussed in Section 2, initially appears to have intended to market her books as young adult before being caught up in the boom). However, on this list, 21 of the 100 books have been shelved as 'young adult'. A further 5 have been shelved as 'young adult > high school', and none of these overlap with the 'young adult' label, which means that approximately a quarter of these books have been identified as young adult by readers. The links between young adult and new adult during the boom period became tenuous, as new adult shifted from being a genre defined primarily by intended readership to one defined by plot. This list suggests that those links are perhaps firming up again.

Table 9 Goodreads genre shelf labels for top 100 books on Goodreads most read this week in new adult list, as of 2 June 2020

Goodreads Genre Shelf Label	Number of Times Applied to Corpus
Academic > college	4
Adult	2
Contemporary	46
Contemporary romance > sports romance	2
Dark	2
Fairies > fae	1
Fantasy	28
Fantasy > magic	4
Fantasy > paranormal	3
Fantasy > urban fantasy	3
Fiction	17
Historical > historical fiction	1
Mystery	3
New adult	23
Novella	1
Paranormal > demons	1
Paranormal > shapeshifters	1
Polyamorous > reverse harem	1
Romance	84
Romance > contemporary romance	24
Science fiction > dystopia	3
Sports > sports	7
Thriller	2
Westerns	2
Women's fiction > chick lit	5

Table 9 Cont.

Goodreads Genre Shelf Label	Number of Times Applied to Corpus
Young adult	21
Young adult > high school	5
Young adult > young adult fantasy	1

Finally, as with the Amazon lists, we can see again a decline in the use of the genre label 'new adult'. All of the books on the list had been shelved as new adult; however, in only twenty-three did the term appear in the top three genre shelf labels. This may be indicative of several things. The most obvious is that the term is falling into obsolescence. This would seem to be mirrored by the decline in book numbers that can be observed in FictionDB. However, it may also indicate that the genre is in a period of flux. The centre of the fuzzy set – first person contemporary romance between college-aged protagonists – seems to have remained strong. However, the decline in the use of the term 'new adult' seen in the Amazon lists may indicate that other terms, such as 'contemporary romance' (which has historically tended to apply to third-person contemporary romance novels), may eventually subsume 'new adult' as generic descriptors for these texts. The generic diversification on the borders of the fuzzy set seem to show that new adult is in a period of change and evolution, as those borders begin to encroach on the centre.

Simply put, new adult seems to be having an identity crisis. As Sections 1 and 2 have shown, this is not the first identity crisis that it has had. From its first crisis, after the St Martin's competition and the roadblock posed by the physical shelf, came the boom, which crystallised the fuzzy set's centre. As the boom receded, and the genre faded from mainstream visibility, so came this second crisis. 'Crisis' generally brings with it negative connotations, and certainly, from an economic standpoint, the recession of the genre from mainstream literary consciousness would have had a notable impact. However, these same logics put the genre – as they do all genres – in a position where adaptation and evolution are not just possible but mandatory, if it is to survive.

The ways in which readers are beginning to shelve books from genres outside romance – most notably, fantasy – as new adult indicates that this evolution is in process – for social formations, if not quite yet for institutions. Interestingly, after crystallising as a genre label for a specific form of romance novel, the ways in which readers are understanding and mobilising the term 'new adult' seems to be aligning increasingly with the way the term was initially intended to be understood and mobilised: as a descriptor for a generic melting pot of texts.

To unpack this further: Table 10 includes the top ten books on the Goodreads 'most read this week in new adult' list and its top Goodreads genre shelf labels.

This list is a neat illustration of the current state of flux in new adult fiction, encompassing where it has been and where it might go. We have several books that fit the boom definition of new adult: *Looking to Score*, for instance, clearly hits all three identifying features (contemporary romance, college-aged protagonists, first person), as can be seen in this excerpt from the blurb:

> I have plans to graduate a semester early, and nothing or no one will get in my way. I'm a Virgo, after all. Oakley Davis might be a privileged, cocky football star, but I'm Amanda Matthews, and I'll do whatever it takes to get my A.
>
> I just have to make sure I don't end up falling in love with the idiot, first. (Gray & June 2020)

However, several books on the list do not meet the boom definition at all. The three books by Sarah J. Maas are in the first person and feature a nineteen-year-old heroine (i.e. college-aged), but they are clearly not contemporary romance: they are high-fantasy books set in a faerie court. Moreover, despite the age of the heroine, they have been widely marketed as and institutionally classified as young adult. The list also includes books that depart from the boom definition in other ways: for example, *By a Thread* is a first-person contemporary romance novel, but the heroine is thirty-nine

Table 10 Top ten books on Goodreads most read this week in new adult list, as of 2 June 2020

Title	Author	Publisher	Goodreads Label #1	Goodreads Label #2	Goodreads Label #3
By a Thread	Score, Lucy	That's What She Said (micropress)	Romance	Romance > contemporary romance	Contemporary
Verity	Hoover, Colleen	Hoover Ink (self-published)	Thriller	Romance	Mystery
IOU	Marie, Kristy	Self-published (enrolled in Kindle Unlimited)	Academic > college	New adult	Romance
The Unhoneymooners	Lauren, Christina	Gallery Books	Romance	Contemporary	Fiction
A Court of Thorns and Roses	Maas, Sarah J.	Bloomsbury	Fantasy	Young adult	Romance
A Court of Mist and Fury	Maas, Sarah J.	Bloomsbury	Fantasy	Romance	Young adult
Riot House	Hart, Callie	Self-published (enrolled in Kindle Unlimited)	Romance	New adult	Dark

Looking to Score	Gray, Carrie and June, Coralee	Self-published (enrolled in Kindle Unlimited)	Academic > college	Sports > sports	Romance
My Favorite Souvenir	Ward, Penelope and Keeland, Vi	C. Scott Publishing (self-published, enrolled in Kindle Unlimited)	Romance	Romance > contemporary romance	Contemporary
A Court of Wings and Ruin	Maas, Sarah J.	Bloomsbury	Fantasy	Romance	Young adult

years old, and thus a long way outside the emerging adult who was the initial intended market of new adult. New adult stalwart Colleen Hoover has a book on the list, but it is a notable departure from her books that appeared on the list during the boom: *Verity* is a psychological thriller.

In short: in terms of textual content, not a great many patterns can be observed on this list, beyond the fact that the boundaries of the fuzzy set are beginning to notably encroach on the centre, thus making the set even fuzzier than it was before. If we examine publication, there are some clearer trends evident, but they do not tell us much beyond the fact that books do not currently appear to be be marketed and sold as new adult by traditional publishers. At the very least, this is true of the books on this list: Sarah J. Maas' books are marketed as young adult fantasy and Christina Lauren's as adult romantic comedy. The centre of the fuzzy set remains clearer in the self-publishing space, especially in Kindle Unlimited (which was also made clear by the Amazon bestseller lists). However, self-publishing is also a space where boundaries can be pushed and the centre encroached upon: Colleen Hoover's return to self-publishing and move to a different plot-based genre is a good example of that.

I have claimed elsewhere that 'new adult' has come to refer mostly to a specific form of focalisation; that is, first person, usually alternating perspectives between protagonists (2018a, 15). I made this claim in 2018, and while I do not believe it is now entirely incorrect, the present-day incarnation of new adult has become fuzzier again. This form of focalisation belongs to the centre, but, as I have discussed in this section, the edges of the fuzzy set are becoming fuzzier, and there are increasing numbers of incursions from the boundaries. New adult is in the midst of an identity crisis. It may still predominantly refer to first-person contemporary romance novels, but that definition – per Attebery (1992), the definition of the centre of the fuzzy set – is being increasingly troubled. Many of these boundary books troubling the centre adhere to St Martin's definition of new adult; however, even some of the admittedly loose restrictions placed on this generic melting pot are not being upheld (for example, protagonist age no longer seems to be as tightly restricted to the 18–25 demographic). As new adult moves into the future and continues to develop, and as readers continue to mobilise the term in different ways, it is not at all certain that the current generic centre will hold.

Conclusion

In this Element, I have offered the most detailed account currently available of the emergence, explosion of popularity, and contemporaneous state of new adult fiction. This is, I contend, an account that is of interest on its own merits. While the fortunes of new adult have fluctuated over the past decade or so, the genre label itself has had a notable amount of staying power, and I have no doubt that the category will continue to develop and reshape itself going forward.

Where I would like to conclude, however, is not with a set of predictions about where new adult might go next, but with some thoughts on what this account of new adult's brief but tumultuous history can tell us about genre and how it operates in the contemporary literary marketplace. As my account of new adult's evolution has shown, genre is in no way fixed. Even in a short amount of time, what a genre label refers to can develop and change extremely rapidly. Genre is a process, not a static phenomenon (Fletcher et al. 2018; Wilkins 2005). Therefore, what do we need to take into account when discussing genre in the marketplace?

In answer to this question, I propose the following four considerations:

1. *Treat definitions with caution.* David Fishelov defines genre as 'a combination of prototypical, representative members, and a flexible set of constitute rules that apply to some levels of literary texts, to some individual writers, usually to more than one literary period, and to more than one language and culture' (2010, 8). There is a considerable amount of flexibility built into this definition – Fishelov is clearly not approaching genres as fixed phenomena – but I contend it perhaps does not go far enough (it is, in itself, a definition we should be cautious of). As the case of new adult shows, what a genre label signifies can change an extraordinary amount in a very short space of time. The contemporary publishing industry moves incredibly quickly. Although the object of the print book has defied expectations in its staying power, the emergence of digital media and fora for publishing has ensured that the speed at which the industry moves – and thus the speed at which genre develops – has been exponentially accelerated in the twenty-first century. The modern genre scholar needs to be aware of the speed of this

process and account for the problem of 'immediate obsolescence' that accompanies the study of contemporary publishing (Thompson 2012, xi). This is true especially when trying to satisfy the scholarly impulse to define the field of study – in this case, a genre. Marie-Laure Ryan argues the following:

> [T]he concept of genre will only receive a firm theoretical basis if the investigator confronts the questions which underlie every taxonomical enterprise: Why classify? What is to be classified? How is one to classify? As long as these questions are shunned, discourse about genre will be not theory, but simply criticism. (1981, 110)

These are questions I suggest that all scholars of genre should consider closely, especially when trying to mount definitions. The case of new adult shows that genres 'in the wild', so to speak, are rarely clearly defined: rather, they are fuzzy sets (Attebery 1992; Ryan 1981). As Ryan contends, this fuzziness should be a matter to account for rather than a problem to solve through the application of rigid external taxonomy. We should be wary of this rigidity in scholarly definitions of genres previously mounted and resist the urge to apply it to any new definitions we develop.

2.   *Genres are marketing categories.* I began this Element with an extended meditation on the differences – or lack thereof – between the concepts of 'genre' and 'category'. While there are spheres where the two can be productively differentiated, for the most part, I contend that they are virtually synonymous. Whether a category is determined primarily by plot trajectory, other narrative features, intended audience or some other reason is virtually irrelevant in institutional spaces where genre classifications are applied, such as bookshops or libraries, and for the most part in spaces like Goodreads, where consumers develop their own folksonomical practices. The logics behind determining whether a text belongs to a given category might be different, but the logics behind how these categories operate are the same, in that the genre label enables texts to be found by readers who are seeking out that genre. In addition, as this Element has shown, there can be substantial

shifts in what these genre labels mean and how a text's belonging to that genre is determined: over the course of only a few years, new adult moved from being a category defined primarily by intended audience to one defined primarily by narrative elements. Claire Squires describes genre as 'a crucial component in the marketplace, as it is one of the primary means by which authors and readers communicate' (2007, 70). I suggest that this communication between different aspects of the genre world is one of the most interesting spheres for the study of genre going forward. If we can move past – or, at least, sidestep – some of these questions about what genre is and is not (noting, as I stated earlier, that we should be very wary of fixed definitions in this space), then we can open up extremely productive questions about how genre operates.

3. *Industrial and social factors should be part of any account of genre.* I have been informed in my approach to new adult by the concept of the 'genre world' as outlined by Lisa Fletcher, Beth Driscoll and Kim Wilkins, who argue that the constitutive factors of this world are 'a sector of the publishing industry, a social formation, and a body of texts' (2018, 997). As they note, studies of genre have generally privileged the last (2018, 997), with structural and/or morphological approaches dominating (Duff 2014). However, as my exploration of the development of new adult has shown, studying texts alone to interrogate genre is not sufficient: while it might be interesting, it misses much of the story. The publishing industry played an enormous part in the development of new adult through the St Martin's contest and its acquisition of self-published bestsellers, while social formations, such as the Goodreads user community, drove the development of the new adult fiction of the boom. If we are to understand the operations of genre fully – to understand it as a process shaped by the interactions of authors, readers, institutions and texts rather than as a fixed and static phenomenon (Wilkins 2005) – it is imperative that we take into account not just the texts themselves but also the conditions and circumstances of their production and reception (Squires 2007, 7).

4. *The study of genre is the study of paratext.* Paratext is not the sole factor in determining a text's genre; however, it is a key object of study for scholars seeking to avoid some of the overtly structural, strictly text-

based approaches of the past. Both peritexts and epitexts play key roles in establishing a text's belonging to a specific generic category. The generic category in which a publisher seeks to market a text is often clearly evident in peritext, in cover design and copy, frontmatter and backmatter and thus can open up potential areas of study into the industrial aspects of genre. Epitext is, I contend, perhaps even more vital an area of study, as it encompasses things like a book's shelving in both institutional spaces like bookshops and social spaces like Goodreads. The study of texts can help us investigate what is in that text, but the study of paratext can help us investigate how that text is both intended to be and actually understood. If, as Amy Devitt argues, genre is 'a classification that people make as they use symbols to get along in the world' (2004, 8), then paratext in all its forms gives us a useful way in to beginning to understand what those symbols mean and how they operate.

New adult fiction is an especially interesting case study to demonstrate the importance of these considerations, because it is in many ways not legible if we do not take them into account. It is not possible to provide a single definition of new adult, even though the category is only about a decade old. Indeed, elsewhere, I attempted to define it at three different points – diachronic definitions rather than a static one – and even this could not really adequately capture the category's fluidity (McAlister 2018a). Its development from a category determined primarily by intended audience to one determined by plot features (and then potentially back again) demonstrates the nebulousness of a genre's constituent factors and how swiftly they can change and develop. This development is impossible to account for without interrogation of the industrial and social backgrounds; the study of the genre's paratexts – especially its epitexts – is one of the best ways in which we can approach this. However, these considerations are not unique to the study of new adult. They can be used, I contend, to better understand and interrogate the roles and evolutions of many other genres in the contemporary literary marketplace, and, beyond that, the roles and evolutions of genre more broadly.

References

AJ. (2012). 'Review of *Hopeless*'. Goodreads, 24 June 2012, www
.goodreads.com/review/show/354663307?book_show_action=false&
from_review_page=2. Accessed 16 June 2020.

Albrechtslund, A. (2019). 'Amazon, Kindle, and Goodreads: Implications
for Literary Consumption in the Digital Age'. *Consumption Markets and
Culture*, published online first. doi: 10.1080/10253866.2019.1640216.

Amazon. (2020). 'Amazon Best Sellers in New Adult and College
Romance'. Amazon, 2 June 2020, www.amazon.com/Best-Sellers-
Kindle-Store-New-Adult-College-Romance/zgbs/digital-text
/6487838011. Accessed 2 June 2020.

Anderson, E. K. (2012). 'Guest Post from Nora Zelevansky on the "New
Adult" Market'. *Write All the Words!* 18 July 2012, www
.ekristinanderson.com/?p=4028. Accessed 16 June 2020.

Andriani, L. (2009). 'Weiss to St Martin's'. *Publisher's Weekly*,
5 November 2009, www.publishersweekly.com/pw/by-topic/industry-
news/people/article/28519-weiss-to-st-martin-s.html. Accessed 16 June
2020.

Arnett, J. J. (2000). 'Emerging Adulthood: A Theory of Development from
the Late Teens Through the Twenties'. *American Psychologist*, 55(5),
469–80. doi: 10.1037/0003-066X.55.5.469.

Associated Press. (2013). 'Self-Published Star Colleen Hoover, Author of
Hopeless, Has Book Deal'. *Global News*, 22 January 2013, https://
globalnews.ca/news/381833/self-published-star-colleen-hoover-author
-of-hopeless-has-book-deal/. Accessed 16 June 2020.

Attebery, B. (1992). *Strategies of Fantasy*, Bloomington: Indiana University
Press.

Baker, K. J. M. (2012). '"New Adult" Fiction Is Now an Official Literary
Genre Because Marketers Want Us to Buy Things'. *Jezebel*, 15

November 2012, jezebel.com/5960942/new-adult-fiction-is-now-an-offi cial-literary-genre-because-marketers-want-you-to-buy-things. Accessed 16 June 2020.

Bao, T. & Chang, T. L. S. (2014). 'Why Amazon Uses Both the *New York Times* Best Seller List and Customer Reviews: An Empirical Study of Multiplier Effects on Product Sales from Multiple Earned Media'. *Decision Support Systems*, 67, 1–8. doi: 10.1016/j.dss.2014.07.004.

Barnett, T. (2015). 'Platforms for Social Reading: Material Imagery in Digital Book Formats'. *Scholarly and Research Communication*, 6(4), 1–23. doi: 10.22230/src.2015v6n4a211.

Becker, H. S. (2008 [1982]). *Art Worlds*, 25th Anniversary Edn, Berkeley: University of California Press, www.ucpress.edu/book/978052025636 1/art-worlds-25th-anniversary-edition

Biggs Waller, S. (2014). *A Mad Wicked Folly*, New York: Viking.

Binks, D. (2014). 'Young Adult Literature: Genre Is Not Readership'. *Kill Your Darlings*, 9 December 2014, www.killyourdarlings.com.au/2014/12/ young-adult-literature-genre-is-not-readership/. Accessed 16 June 2020.

BISG. 'BISAC Subject Codes'.(n.d.), Book Industry Study Group, https://bisg.org/page/BISACSubjectCodes/. Accessed 16 June 2020.

Brookover, S., Burns, L. & Jensen, K. (2013). 'What's New About New Adult?' *The Horn Book*, 17 December, www.hbook.com/2013/12/choos ing-books/horn-book-magazine/whats-new-about-new-adult/. Accessed 16 June 2020.

Brown, D. W. (2011). 'How Young Adult Fiction Came of Age'. *The Atlantic*, 1 August 2011, www.theatlantic.com/entertainment/archive/ 2011/08/how-young-adult-fiction-came-of-age/242671/. Accessed 16 June 2020.

Burgess, G. (2013). *Brooklyn Girls*, New York: St Martin's Griffin.

Carmack, C. (2012). 'The One About What New Adult Means to Me'. *Cora Carmack Books*, 12 November 2012, coracarmack.blogspot.com.au

/2012/11/the-one-about-what-new-adult-means-to-me.html. Accessed 16 June 2020.

Carson, R. (2011). *The Girl of Fire and Thorns*, New York: Greenwillow.

Clute, J. (1997). 'Fantasy'. *Encyclopedia of Fantasy*, http://sf-encyclopedia .uk/fe.php?nm=fantasy. Accessed 2 February 2021.

Davis, M. (2020). 'Five Processes in the Platformisation of Cultural Production: Amazon and Its Publishing Ecosystem'. *Australian Humanities Review*, 66, 83–104.

Deahl, R. (2012a). 'Atria Inks Self Pub'd Bestseller McGuire to Two-Book Deal'. *Publishers Weekly*, 11 July, www.publishersweekly.com/pw/by-topic/industry-news/industry-deals/article/52953-atria-inks-self-pub -d-bestseller-mcguire-to-two-book-deal.html. Accessed 16 June 2020.

Deahl, R. (2012b). 'Penguin Divisions Team Up to Buy Self-Pubbed Bestseller "Easy"'. *Publishers Weekly*, 4 October, www.publishersweekly.com/pw/ by-topic/authors/pw-select/article/54223-penguin-divisions-team-up-to-buy-self-pubbed-bestseller-easy.html. Accessed 16 June 2020.

Desrochers, N., LaPlante, A., Martin, K., Quan-Haase, A. & Spiteri, L. (2016). 'Illusions of a "Bond": Tagging Cultural Products Across Online Platforms'. *Journal of Documentation*, 72(6), 1027–51. doi: 10.1108/JD-09-2015-0110.

Desrochers, N., Quan-Haase, A., Pennington, D. R., LaPlante, A., Martin, K. & Spiteri, L. (2013). 'Beyond the Playlist: Looking at User-Generated Collocation of Cultural Products Through Social Tagging'. *Proceedings of the Association for Information Science and Technology*, 50(1), 1–4. doi: 10.1002/meet.14505001014.

Devitt, A. (2004). *Writing Genres*, Carbondale: Southern Illinois University Press.

Doll, J. (2012). 'What Does "Young Adult" Mean?' *The Atlantic*, 19 April, www.theatlantic.com/culture/archive/2012/04/what-does-young-adult-mean/329105/. Accessed 16 June 2020.

Duff, D. (2014). 'Introduction'. In D. Duff, ed., *Modern Genre Theory*, Abingdon, UK: Routledge, 1–24.

Elle. (2012). 'Review of *Point of Retreat*'. *Goodreads*, 5 April 2012, www.goodreads.com/review/show/307213977?book_show_action=false&from_review_page=6. Accessed 16 June 2020.

Engberg, G. (2014). 'What Is New Adult Fiction?' *Booklist Online*, August, www.booklistonline.com/What-Is-New-Adult-Fiction-Gillian-Engberg/pid=6918519. Accessed 16 June 2020.

Ferriss, S. & Young, M. (2013). *Chick Lit: The New Woman's Fiction*, New York: Routledge.

FictionDB. (n.d.). Database, www.fictiondb.com/. Accessed 27 May 2020.

Fielding, H. (1996). *Bridget Jones' Diary*, London: Penguin.

Fishelov, D. (2010 [1993]). *Metaphors of Genre: The Role of Analogies in Genre Theory*, University Park: University of Pennsylvania Press.

Fletcher, L., Driscoll, B. & Wilkins, K. (2018). 'Genre Worlds and Popular Fiction: The Case of Twenty-First-Century Australian Romance'. *Journal of Popular Culture*, 51(4), 997–1015. doi: 10.1111/jpcu.12706.

Fletcher, L. & McAlister, J. (2019). 'The Paratextuality of Category Romance: The Branding of Short Shelf Life Fiction'. Paper presented at the Popular Culture Association annual conference, Washington, DC.

Forman, G. (2011). *Where She Went*, New York: Dutton.

Frow, J. (2014 [2006]). *Genre*, 2nd edn, Abingdon, UK: Routledge.

Genette, G. (1997 [1987]). *Paratexts: Thresholds of Interpretation*, trans. J. E. Lewin, Cambridge: Cambridge University Press.

Gerrard, N. (1989). *Into the Mainstream*, London: Pandora.

Gold, T. (2016). 'What Is New Adult Literature?' *The Librarian Who Doesn't Say Shhh!* 25 April, librarianwhodoesntsayshhh.com/2016/04/25/new-adult-literature/. Accessed 16 June 2020.

Gomez, H. (2013). 'ALA 2013: New Adult Fiction: What Is It, and Is It Really Happening?' *The Hub – YALSA*, 9 July 2013, www.yalsa.ala.org

/thehub/2013/07/09/ala-2013-new-adult-fiction-what-is-it-and-is-it-really-happening/. Accessed 16 June 2020.

Goodreads. (n.d.). Database, www.goodreads.com/. Accessed 27 May 2020.

Goris, A. (2013). 'Happily Ever After . . . And After: Serialisation and the Popular Romance Novel'. *Americana: The Journal of American Popular Culture*, 12(1), www.americanpopularculture.com/journal/articles/spring_2013/goris.htm. Accessed 16 June 2020.

Gray, C. & June, C. (2020). *Looking to Score*, n.p.: self-published.

Halverson, D. (2014). *Writing New Adult Fiction*, New York: Penguin.

Hannah. (2012). 'Review of *Slammed*'. *Goodreads*, 15 March 2012, www.goodreads.com/review/show/294982797?book_show_action=false&from_review_page=2. Accessed 16 June 2020.

Hoffman, K. (2010). 'New Adult: What Is it?' *Writer's Digest*, 7 January 2010, www.writersdigest.com/editor-blogs/guide-to-literary-agents/new-adult-what-is-it. Accessed 16 June 2020.

Hoffman, K. (2010). *Twenty-Somewhere*, n.p.: self-published.

Hoover, C. (2012). 'What's *Slammed* About Anyway?' *Colleen Hoover*, 2012, colleenhoover.com/slammed. Accessed via the Wayback Machine, 16 June 2020.

Hoover, C. (2012). *Hopeless*, n.p.: self-published.

Hoover, C. (2012). *Point of Retreat*, n.p.: self-published.

Hoover, C. (2012). *Slammed*, n.p.: self-published.

Hoover, C. (2013). *Losing Hope*, New York: Atria Books.

Hoover, C. (2013). *This Girl*, New York: Atria Books.

Hoover, C. (2014). *Maybe Someday*, New York: Atria Books.

Hoover, C. (2014). *Ugly Love*, New York: Atria Books.

Hoover, C. (2015). *November 9*, New York: Atria Books.

Hoover, C. (2018). *Verity*, n.p.: Hoover Ink.

Hoover, C. (2020). 'About Colleen Hoover', *Colleen Hoover*, 2020, www.colleenhoover.com/about-coho/. Accessed 16 June 2020.

Jae, A. (2014). 'Young Adult vs. New Adult: What's the Difference?' *Writability*, March 2014, avajae.blogspot.com.au/2014/03/young-adult-vs-new-adult.html. Accessed 16 June 2020.

Jae-Jones, S. (2009a). 'St Martin's New Adult Contest'. *Uncreated Conscience*, 9 November 2009, sjaejones.com/blog/2009/st-martins-new-adult-contest/. Accessed via the Wayback Machine, 16 June 2020.

Jae-Jones, S. (2009b). 'Postadolescent or "New Adult" Fiction'. *Uncreated Conscience*, 10 November 2009, sjaejones.com/blog/2009/postadoles cent-or-new-adult-fiction/. Accessed via the Wayback Machine, 16 June 2020.

Jae-Jones, S. (2009c). 'New Adult & Shelving'. *Uncreated Conscience*, 13 November 2009, sjaejones.com/blog/2009/new-adult-shelving/. Accessed via the Wayback Machine, 16 June 2020.

Jae-Jones, S. (2009d). 'You Won! Happy Thanksgiving!' *Uncreated Conscience*, 26 November 2009, sjaejones.com/blog/2009/you-won-happy-thanksgiving/. Accessed via the Wayback Machine, 16 June 2020.

Jae-Jones, S. (2009e). 'New Adult Is Not Necessarily Chick Lit'. *Uncreated Conscience*, 10 December 2009, sjaejones.com/blog/2009/new-adult-is-not-necessarily-chicklit/. Accessed via the Wayback Machine, 16 June 2020.

Jae-Jones, S. (2011). 'What We've Acquired Thus Far'. *Uncreated Conscience*, 18 January 2011, sjaejones.com/blog/2011/what-weve-acquired-thus-far/. Accessed via the Wayback Machine, 16 June 2020.

James, E. L. (2011). *Fifty Shades of Grey*, New York: Vintage.

Jameson, F. (1975). 'Magical Narratives: Romance as Genre'. *New Literary History*, 7(1), 135–63. doi: 10.2307/468283.

Jensen, K. (2019). 'Do Teens Get Pushed Out of YA Books When It's Called a Genre?' *Book Riot*, 29 March 2019, https://bookriot.com/2019/03/29/ya-is-not-a-genre/. Accessed 16 June 2020.

Kaufman, L. (2012). 'Beyond Wizards and Vampires to Sex'. *New York Times*, 22 December 2012, www.nytimes.com/2012/12/22/books/

young-adult-authors-add-steaminess-to-their-tales.html. Accessed 16 June 2020.

Kephart, B. (2012). 'On Publishing for Gen Y and "New Adult" Literature'. *Publishing Perspectives*, 26 November 2012, publishingperspectives.com/2012/11/on-publishing-for-gen-y-and-new-adult-literature/. Accessed 16 June 2020.

Keplinger, K. (2010). *The Duff*, New York: Little, Brown.

Kieffer, K. (2017). 'What Is New Adult Fiction?' *Well-Storied*, 21 July 2017, www.well-storied.com/blog/what-is-new-adult-fiction. Accessed 16 June 2020.

Kinsella, S. (2000). *Secret Dreamworld of a Shopaholic*, London: Transworld.

Kole, M. (2011). 'New Adult and College-Aged YA Protagonists'. *KidLit*, 30 November 2011, kidlit.com/2011/11/30/college-aged-ya-protagonists/. Accessed 16 June 2020.

Korda, M. (2001). *Making the List: A Cultural History of the American Bestseller, 1900–1999*, New York: Barnes & Noble Books.

Lauren, C. (2019). *The Unhoneymooners*, New York: Gallery Books.

Leighton, M. (2012). *Down to You*. n.p.: self-published.

Long, R. F. (2012). *The Treachery of Beautiful Things*, New York: Dial Books.

Maas, S. (2015). *Court of Thorns and Roses*, New York: Bloomsbury.

Maas, S. (2016). *Court of Mist and Fury*, New York: Bloomsbury.

Maas, S. (2017). *Court of Wings and Ruin*, New York: Bloomsbury.

Macmillan. 'Sweet Valley Confidential: Ten Years Later'. Macmillan Publishers, n.d., https://us.macmillan.com/sweetvalleyconfidential/francinepascal/9781429965200. Accessed 16 June 2020.

McAlister, J. (2018a). 'Defining and Redefining Popular Genres: The Evolution of "New Adult" Fiction'. *Australian Literary Studies*, 33(4), 1–19. doi: 10.20314/als.0fd566d109.

McAlister, J. (2018b). 'Messy Multiplicity: Strategies for Serialisation in "New Adult" Fiction'. In A. Parey, ed., *Prequels, Coquels, and Sequels in Contemporary Anglophone Fiction*, Abingdon, UK: Routledge, 142–62.

McAlister, J. (2020). 'Erotic Romance'. In J. Kamblé, E. Selinger & H. M. Teo, eds., *The Routledge Companion to Popular Romance Fiction*, Abingdon, UK: Routledge, 212–28.

McBride, G. (2009a). 'St Martin's Press Has New Publisher and Good News for YA Writers'. *Georgia McBride*, 5 November 2009a, georgiamcbride-books.wordpress.com:80/2009/11/05/st-martins-press-has-new-publis her-and-good-news-for-ya-writers/. Accessed via the Wayback Machine, 16 June 2020.

McBride, G. (2009b). 'Interview: JJ, St Martin's Press Editorial Assistant'. *Georgia McBride*, 9 November 2009, georgiamcbridebooks.wordpress.com/2009/11/09/interview-jj-st-martins-press-editorial-assistant/. Accessed via the Wayback Machine, 16 June 2020.

McBride, G. (2009c). 'St Martin's Press "New Adult" Submissions Contest Sponsored by #YAlitchat'. *Georgia McBride*, 9 November 2009, georgiamcbridebooks.wordpress.com:80/2009/11/09/st-martins-press-new -adult-submissions-contest-sponsored-by-yalitchat/. Accessed via the Wayback Machine, 16 June 2020.

McBride, G. (2009d). 'St Martin's Press Contest: How It All Went Down'. *Georgia McBride*, 27 November 2009, georgiamcbridebooks. wordpress.com:80/2009/11/27/st-martins-press-contest-how-it-all-went-down/. Accessed via the Wayback Machine, 16 June 2020.

McBride, G. (2009e). 'SMP Winners: What I Really Think (About You)'. *Georgia McBride*, 1 December 2009, georgiamcbridebooks.wordpress.com/80/2009/12/01/smp-winners-what-i-really-think-about-you/. Accessed via the Wayback Machine, 16 June 2020.

McCracken, E. (2013). 'Expanding Genette's Epitext/Peritext Model for Transitional Electronic Literature: Centrifugal and Centripetal Vectors

on Kindles and iPads'. *Narrative* 21(1), 105–24. doi: 10.1353/
nar.2013.0005.

McGuire, J. (2011). '*Beautiful Disaster*: A Novel', www.jamiemcguire.com
/beautiful-disaster/. Accessed via the Wayback Machine, 16 June 2020.

McGuire, J. (2012b). 'FAQ', www.jamiemcguire.com/index.php?
option=com_content&view=article&id=87&itemid=27/. Accessed
via the Wayback Machine, 5 February 2021.

McGuire, J. (2013). *A Beautiful Wedding*, New York: Atria Books.

McGuire, J. (2013). *Walking Disaster*, New York: Atria Books.

McGuire, J. (2014). *Beautiful Oblivion*, New York: Atria Books.

McGuire, J. (2020). 'About Jamie', www.jamiemcguire.com/bio. Accessed
16 June 2020.

Mead, R. (2009). 'The Gossip Mill'. *The New Yorker*, 19 October 2009, www
.newyorker.com/magazine/2009/10/19/the-gossip-mill. Accessed 16
June 2020.

Mead, R. (2011). *Bloodlines*, New York: Razorbill.

Meadows, J. (2009). 'Interview with S. Jae-Jones on New Adult'. *(W)ords
and (W)ardances*, 18 November 2009, jmeadows.livejournal.com/
725113.html. Accessed via the Wayback Machine, 16 June 2020.

Missler, H. (2016). *The Cultural Politics of Chick Lit: Popular Fiction,
Postfeminism and Representation*, Abingdon, UK: Routledge.

Monika. (2011). Review of *Beautiful Disaster*. Goodreads, 10 June, www
.goodreads.com/review/show/175458280?book_show_action=false&
from_review_page=2. Accessed 16 June 2020.

Moore, P. (2013). 'An Interview with Gemma Burgess, Author of *Brooklyn
Girls*'. 4 July 2013, www.philippamoore.net/book-ends/2013/07/04/an-
interview-with-gemma-burgess-author-of-brooklyn-girls. Accessed 16
June 2020.

Moretti, F. (2005). *Graphs, Maps and Trees: Abstract Models for a Literary
History*, London & New York: Verso.

Moretti, F. (2013). *Distant Reading*. London & New York: Verso.

Motter, V. (2011). 'More Questions for the Agent: New Adult'. *Navigating the Slush Pile*, 5 July, navigatingtheslushpile.blogspot.com.au/2011/07/more-questions-for-agent-new-adult.html. Accessed 16 June 2020.

Murray, S. (2015). 'Charting the Digital Literary Sphere'. *Contemporary Literature*, 56(2), 311–39.

Murray, S. (2019). 'Secret Agents: Algorithmic Culture, Goodreads and Datafication of the Contemporary Book World'. *European Journal of Cultural Studies*, published online first. doi: 10.1177/1367549419886026.

Nakamura, L. (2013). '"Words with Friends": Socially Networked Reading on Goodreads'. *PMLA*, 128(1), 238–43.

Narula, S. K. (2014). 'Millions of People Reading Alone, Together: The Rise of Goodreads'. *The Atlantic*, 12 February, www.theatlantic.com/entertainment/archive/2014/02/millions-of-people-reading-alone-together-the-rise-of-goodreads/283662/. Accessed 16 June 2020.

Naughton, J. (2014). 'New Adult Matures'. *Publishers Weekly*, 261(28), 20–6.

Nelson, K. (2009). 'New Line at SMP'. *PubRants*, 7 December, https://pubrants.blogspot.com/2009/12/new-line-at-smp.html. Accessed via the Wayback Machine, 16 June 2020.

Nelson, K. (2013). 'New Adult – Perhaps the Latest Word for Chick Lit'. *Nelson Agency*, 17 April, https://nelsonagency.com/2013/04/new-adult-perhaps-the-latest-word-for-chick-lit/. Accessed 16 June 2020.

New York Times. (n.d.). 'Combined Print and E-Book Fiction – Bestsellers', 2012–2020, www.nytimes.com/books/best-sellers/combined-print-and-e-book-fiction/. Accessed 27 May 2020.

New York Times. (n.d.). 'E-Book Fiction – Bestsellers, 2012–2020, www.nytimes.com/books/best-sellers/e-book-fiction/. Accessed via the Wayback Machine, 27 May 2020.

New York Times. (n.d.). 'Paperback Trade Fiction – Bestsellers', 2012–2020, www.nytimes.com/books/best-sellers/trade-fiction-paperback/. Accessed 27 May 2020.

Nodelman, P. (2008). *The Hidden Adult: Defining Children's Literature*, Baltimore, MD: Johns Hopkins University Press.

Park, J. (2011). *Flat-Out Love*, n.p.: self-published.

Pascal, F. (2013). *Sweet Valley Confidential*, New York: St Martin's Griffin.

Pattee, A. (2011). *Reading the Adolescent Romance:* Sweet Valley High *and the Popular Young Adult Romance Novel*, New York: Routledge.

Pattee, A. (2017). 'Between Youth and Adulthood: Young Adult and New Adult Literature'. *Children's Literature Association Quarterly*, 42(2), 218–30. doi: 10.1353/chq.2017.0018.

Pattinson, D. (2014). '3 Ways to Know if Your YA Fiction Is Really New Adult Fiction'. *Fiction Notes by Darcy Pattinson*, 13 October, www.darcypattison.com/novels/new-adult/. Accessed 16 June 2020.

Pennington, D. & Spiteri, L. (2018). *Social Tagging for Linking Data Across Environments*, London: Facet.

PT Editors. (2010). 'Now in Hardcover: The Series in 2010'. *Publishing Trends*, 11 May, www.publishingtrends.com/2010/05/now-in-hardcover-the-series-in-2010/. Accessed 16 June 2020.

Redmerski, J. A. (2012). *The Edge of Never*, n.p.: self-published.

Regis, P. (2003). *A Natural History of the Romance Novel*, Philadelphia: University of Pennsylvania Press.

Regis, P. (2011). 'What Do Critics Owe the Romance?' Keynote Address at the Second Annual Conference of the International Association for the Study of Popular Romance'. *Journal of Popular Romance Studies*, 2(1), http://jprstudies.org/2011/10/%e2%80%9cwhat-do-critics-owe-the-romance-keynote-address-at-e2%80%9d-by-pamela-regis/. Accessed 16 June 2020.

Reine, S. M. (2018). *The Tarot Witches I–IV*, New York: Bloomsbury.

RWA. (n.d.). 'About the Romance Genre'. *Romance Writers of America*, n. d., www.rwa.org/Online/Romance_Genre/About_Romance_Genre .aspx. Accessed 16 June 2020.

Ryan, M. (1981). 'Introduction: On the Why, What, and How of Generic Taxonomy'. *Poetics*, 10(2), 109–26. doi: 10.1016/0304-422X(81)90030-9.

Sarner, L. (2013). 'The Problem with New Adult Books'. *Huffington Post*, 14 August, updated 14 October, www.huffingtonpost.com/lauren-sarner /the-problem-with-new-adul_b_3755165.html. Accessed 16 June 2020.

Schmid, W. (2013). 'Implied Reader'. *Living Handbook of Narratology*, 27 January, www.lhn.uni-hamburg.de/contents. Accessed 16 June 2020.

Score, L. (2020). *By a Thread*, n.p.: That's What She Said Publishing.

Smith, S. E. (2012). 'Is "New Adult" Fiction Going to Be a Thing?' *xoJane*, 2 October, www.xojane.com/entertainment/is-new-adult-going-to-be -a-thing. Accessed via the Wayback Machine, 16 June 2020.

Sorensen, A. T. (2007). 'Bestseller Lists and Product Variety'. *The Journal of Industrial Economics*, 55(4), 715–38. doi: 10.1111/j.1467-6451.2007.00327.x.

Sorensen, J. (2012). *The Coincidence of Callie and Kayden*, n.p.: self-published.

Sorensen, J. (2012). *The Secret of Ella and Micha*, n.p.: self-published.

Squires, C. (2007). *Marketing Literature: The Making of Contemporary Writing in Britain*, Basingstoke, UK: Palgrave.

Stearns, M. (2009). '"New Adult" – Specious Category or Market Opportunity?' *Upstart Crow Literary*, 20 November, www.upstartcrowliter ary.com/new-adult-specious-category-or-market-opportunity/. Accessed 16 June 2020.

Stephens, S. C. (2009). *Thoughtless*, n.p.: self-published.

Thompson, J. (2012 [2010]). *The Merchants of Culture: The Publishing Business in the Twenty-First Century*, 2nd edn, Cambridge: Polity.

Todorov, T. & Berrong, R. M. (1976). 'The Origin of Genres'. *New Literary History*, 8(1), 159–70. doi: 10.2307/468619.

Veros, V. (2019). 'Metatextual Conversations: The Exclusion/Inclusion of Genre Fiction in Public Libraries and Social Media Book Groups'. *Journal of the Australian Library and Information Association*, 68(3), 254–67. doi: 10.1080/24750158.2019.1654741.

Webber, T. (2012). *Easy*, n.p.: self-published.

Wendig, C. (2013). '25 Things You Should Know About Young Adult Fiction'. *Terrible Minds*, 4 June, http://terribleminds.com/ramble/2013/06/04/25-things-you-should-know-about-young-adult-fiction/. Accessed 16 June 2020.

West, H. (2014). 'Ask an Editor: Young Adult vs New Adult'. *Swoon Reads*, 28 October, swoonreads.com/blog/ask-an-editor-young-adult-vs-new-adult/. Accessed 16 June 2020.

Westfield, M. (2017). 'In Support of New-Adult Fiction'. *Books by Women*, 12 April, http://booksbywomen.org/in-support-of-new-adult-fiction-by-megan-westfield/. Accessed 16 June 2020.

Wetta, M. (2013). 'What Is New Adult Fiction, Anyway?' *NoveList*, September 2013, www.ebscohost.com/novelist/novelist-special/what-is-new-adult-fiction-anyway. Accessed 16 June 2020.

Wilkins, K. (2005). 'The Process of Genre: Authors, Readers, Institutions'. *Text*, 9(2), www.textjournal.com.au/oct05/wilkins.htm. Accessed 16 June 2020.

Zelevansky, N. (2012). *Semi-Charmed Life*, New York: St Martin's Griffin.

Cambridge Elements ⁼

Publishing and Book Culture

SERIES EDITOR
Samantha Rayner
University College London

Samantha Rayner is a Reader in UCL's Department of
Information Studies. She is also Director of UCL's Centre for
Publishing, co-Director of the Bloomsbury CHAPTER
(Communication History, Authorship, Publishing, Textual
Editing and Reading) and co-editor of the Academic Book of
the Future BOOC (Book as Open Online Content) with UCL
Press.

ASSOCIATE EDITOR
Leah Tether
University of Bristol

Leah Tether is Professor of Medieval Literature and Publishing
at the University of Bristol. With an academic background in
medieval French and English literature and a professional
background in trade publishing, Leah has combined her
expertise and developed an international research profile in
book and publishing history from manuscript to digital.

ABOUT THE SERIES

This series aims to fill the demand for easily accessible, quality texts available for teaching and research in the diverse and dynamic fields of Publishing and Book Culture. Rigorously researched and peer-reviewed Elements will be published under themes, or 'Gatherings'. These Elements should be the first check point for researchers or students working on that area of publishing and book trade history and practice: we hope that, situated so logically at Cambridge University Press, where academic publishing in the UK began, it will develop to create an unrivalled space where these histories and practices can be investigated and preserved.

Cambridge Elements ≡

Publishing and Book Culture

Young Adult Publishing

Gathering Editor: Melanie Ramdarshan Bold

Melanie Ramdarshan Bold is a Senior Lecturer at University College London, where she teaches and researches topics related to Publishing/Book Cultures. Her main research interest centres on developments in authorship, publishing, and reading, and inclusiveness and representation in literary culture, with a focus on books for children and young adults.

ELEMENTS IN THE GATHERING

A full series listing is available at: www.cambridge.org/EPBC

Printed in the United States
by Baker & Taylor Publisher Services